PRAISE FOR

A REPUBLICAN'S LAMENT

"If you are interested in the history of our complex state, you should read Bill Crawford's *A Republican's Lament*. Crawford—a fine writer, experienced political leader, and dedicated education proponent—walks the reader through victories, and disappointments, of our much-loved, and often-maligned, State of Mississippi. Crawford's evocative approach, combined with a journalist's eye, crystalizes a lengthy reluctance to change through courageous leadership."

ROBERT KHAYAT, AUTHOR AND CHANCELLOR EMERITUS AT THE UNIVERSITY OF MISSISSIPPI

"Bill Crawford has preserved a pivotal era in Mississippi political history, and we are in his debt for it. Bill and I viewed the body politic from similar perspectives and often drew differing opinions and took opposing views. But his voice has always been courageous and clarion, and reading his book was a pleasure."

ANDY TAGGART, COAUTHOR OF *MISSISSIPPI POLITICS: THE STRUGGLE FOR POWER, 1976–2008*

"Crawford's book is a must-read, encapsulating largely ignored conservative principles of governance and documenting the emergence and impact of early Republican candidates in Mississippi."

WILLIAM L. WALLER JR., FORMER CHIEF JUSTICE, MISSISSIPPI SUPREME COURT

"Bill Crawford's *A Republican's Lament* shines a light on the shadowy political realm where 'Mississippi's schizophrenia' thrives."

NEIL WHITE, AUTHOR OF *IN THE SANCTUARY OF OUTCASTS*

"This is a wonderful book, [Crawford's] personal experience and command of the 'data' are things no journalist who attempted something like this would have."

LUTHER MUNFORD, LAWYER AND AUTHOR OF *MISSISSIPPI APPELLATE PRACTICE*

"An intellectually curious thinker unafraid of change and discomforting truth, Bill Crawford is a solution-oriented doer."

TERRY WINSTEAD, PAST CHAIRMAN OF THE MISSISSIPPI REAL ESTATE COMMISSION

A REPUBLICAN'S LAMENT

Mississippi Needs Good Government Conservatives

Bill Crawford

Foreword by Lloyd Gray and C. D. Smith

UNIVERSITY PRESS OF MISSISSIPPI / JACKSON

The University Press of Mississippi is the scholarly publishing agency of the Mississippi Institutions of Higher Learning: Alcorn State University, Delta State University, Jackson State University, Mississippi State University, Mississippi University for Women, Mississippi Valley State University, University of Mississippi, and University of Southern Mississippi.

www.upress.state.ms.us

The University Press of Mississippi is a member of the Association of University Presses.

Manufactured in the United States of America
∞

Library of Congress Cataloging-in-Publication Data

Names: Crawford, Bill, (William Sterling), author. | Gray, Lloyd, writer of foreword. | Smith, C. D. Jr., writer of foreword.
Title: A Republican's lament : Mississippi needs good government conservatives / Bill Crawford, Lloyd Gray, C. D. Smith.
Description: Jackson : University Press of Mississippi, 2024. | Includes bibliographical references and index.
Identifiers: LCCN 2024022954 (print) | LCCN 2024022955 (ebook) | ISBN 9781496854421 (hardback) | ISBN 9781496854445 (epub) | ISBN 9781496854452 (epub) | ISBN 9781496854469 (pdf) | ISBN 9781496854476 (pdf)
Subjects: LCSH: Crawford, Bill, (William Sterling)—Political and social views. | Carmichael, Gilbert E.—Influence. | Barbour, Haley, 1947—Influence. | Republican Party (Miss.)—History. | Conservatism—Mississippi—History. | Political campaigns—Mississippi. | Legislators—Mississippi. | Mississippi—Politics and government—1951–
Classification: LCC JK4625 .C73 2024 (print) | LCC JK4625 (ebook) | DDC 320.5209762—dc23/eng/20240611
LC record available at https://lccn.loc.gov/2024022954
LC ebook record available at https://lccn.loc.gov/2024022955

British Library Cataloging-in-Publication Data available

CONTENTS

FOREWORD

LLOYD GRAY AND C. D. SMITH

FEW PEOPLE HAVE HAD A BETTER VIEW OR A WIDER VARIETY OF ROLES in the ups and downs of Mississippi and its communities over the past half century than Bill Crawford. And even fewer have put more of their heart into trying to make this state a better place.

Over the past fifty years, this Canton native has been a daily newspaper reporter, a crusading small-town weekly editor, a statewide political campaign operative, a successful banker, a reform-minded state legislator, an Institutions of Higher Learning (IHL) board leader, an unsuccessful congressional candidate, a community development nonprofit founder and president, a state economic developer, a mentor of developing leaders, and the local community leader most responsible for keeping Naval Air Station Meridian open. Oh, and yes, a statewide syndicated political columnist.

Along the way he became a man of deep and steadfast faith, and that faith has informed and guided his work.

It has not been all sweetness and light. As anyone who has lived in Mississippi for any length of time knows, our progress comes in fits and starts, and often it is one step forward followed by two steps back. Positive change can be painfully slow, and the obstacles—historical and contemporary—are everywhere. Whether it involves making government more efficient, effective, and responsive, providing opportunity for our most needy and vulnerable citizens, or bridging the great racial chasm that has shaped our state's history, the forces of resistance—or just simple inertia—are as strong here as they are anywhere. Bill

Crawford's lifelong mission to help create a new Mississippi has often run headlong into those forces.

Yet remarkably, Bill has persisted, despite the obstacles and the setbacks. Part of that is his stubbornness and headstrong attitude. More important is his core belief that when it gets down to it, the people of Mississippi, with their abundant good-heartedness, neighborliness, kindness, and compassion, will ultimately follow their better nature and the call of the faith that so many of them profess.

This book is a story of one man's struggles and triumphs, his setbacks and his victories, as he sought to make his life a meaningful witness for creating a state where all can flourish. That story parallels a half century in which Mississippi has seen some of its historical highs but also some of its regrettable lows. Bill has been in the middle of many fights, has seen Mississippi history from many vantage points, and has experienced many disappointments: the failure of the modern-day Mississippi Republican Party to be the transforming reformist influence he hoped it could be; the inability of many communities and institutions to sustain progress as leadership changes and factions persist; the still-entrenched racial divisions that keep us from working together to get things done. But just enough has happened to the good over time to keep the flame of hope burning.

Bill Crawford is a conservative—politically, philosophically, intellectually, religiously, and morally—but his conservatism has always carried with it the hope that things can get better for more people, even for those historically left out, if we just put our minds and our energy to the task. His conservatism is not a defense of the status quo nor an angry lashing out at an often perplexing and baffling world, but a belief that applying tested and enduring principles can make life better for everyone. It was once called "compassionate conservatism," a descriptor now largely out of favor but one that captures Bill's world view—and his lifelong vision for Mississippi. He prefers to call it "good government conservatism" in the book.

Readers will find in these pages a reflection of these principles applied to specific challenges Mississippi and its communities have faced over the past fifty years, much of the time unsuccessfully but occasionally with surprising results. They will learn much they didn't know about events familiar and not so familiar to those who have followed the state's political and public life over that time.

Most of all, readers will get to know a deeply devoted Mississippian who longs for his beloved home state to become all that it can be, who has been willing to give his entire working life over to that purpose, and who summons others to take up the cause.

If you know Bill, you know that he is guided in part by the four legacy traits of the late Sonny Montgomery, the consensus-building leader for whom the community development institute Bill founded was named and with whom he had a close friendship. Those traits are faith, fellowship, patriotism, and persistence. You also know that he believes that we are *all* God's children and that we must close the racial divide that continues to exist. It is our hope that this book will inspire others to embrace and work toward Bill's vision of what Mississippi could and should be for future generations.

Lloyd Gray is the executive director of the Phil Hardin Foundation, a statewide education philanthropy based in Meridian. A native Mississippian and Millsaps College graduate, he spent forty years in the newspaper business in Mississippi, interrupted by a brief stint in state government as an assistant secretary of state. He was executive editor of the *Northeast Mississippi Daily Journal* in Tupelo from 1992 until 2015, when he joined the Hardin Foundation.

C. D. Smith is the regional director for AT&T Mississippi, a native Mississippian, and a graduate of Mississippi State University. He is the founding and current chair of The Montgomery Institute and serves on the Board of Trustees for Meridian Community College. A past member of the Mississippi Board of Trustees for State Institutions of Higher Learning, he serves on the Board of Governors for the Mississippi Economic Council and the Board of Commissioners for Weems Mental Health Association.

INTRODUCTION

> Don't you see? This whole land, the whole South, is cursed, and all of us who derive from it, whom it ever suckled, white and black both, lie under the curse.
>
> —ISAAC McCASLIN, WILLIAM FAULKNER'S "THE BEAR" (1935)

INFANT DEATHS, TEEN PREGNANCIES, PERSISTENT POVERTY, FOOD DESerts, gross obesity, homicides, and other such dilemmas portray a Mississippi still cursed eighty-eight years later in 2023.

Nothing has revealed Mississippi's enduring distress more than its multitude of rankings at or near the bottom year after year for these and other dilemmas. A whole array of government systems, leaders, programs, processes, and plans could/should have moved Mississippi upward. But holes in that whole array have kept us sucked to the bottom.

For fifty years since the early 1970s, Republicans have played an ever-increasing role in Mississippi's story. As comedian Jerry Clower might have said, I was amongst 'em. For twenty-five years I held various state and local government and party positions where I participated in the story. For over twenty years I led and participated in civic and nonprofit efforts trying to change the story. And for over fifty-two years I have written columns and op-eds, often controversial, about the story. My friend Lloyd Gray said that my diverse experiences give me a "unique" perspective to write this narrative Maybe. At least I have come to know our holes well.

My perspective was greatly influenced by Gil Carmichael's constructive and moral notions of good government, Haley Barbour's common-sense pragmatism, G. V. "Sonny" Montgomery's faith-based leadership legacy, Dr. Bill Scaggs's example of collaborative servant leadership, the service heritage of my father and grandmother, and my meagre upbringing.

Walk with me as I share my "unique" perspective and writings on the holes in the whole and our need for good government conservatives to stopper them.

A REPUBLICAN'S LAMENT

Chapter One

GOOD GOVERNMENT

THE VISION OF GIL CARMICHAEL

Little did I know that a temporary job in 1975 that started with me driving Gilbert "Gil" Ellzey Carmichael around Mississippi would lead to a lifelong involvement with Republican politics and advocacy of Gil's good government approach to governing.

ONCE UPON A TIME, AN EMERGING REPUBLICAN PARTY LOOKED TO BE a vehicle to lift Mississippi off the bottom. An unlikely source provided the vision. A successful Meridian automobile dealer, Gil Carmichael got involved in Republican politics in the 1960s. In 1963 he served as Lauderdale County chairman for Rubel Phillips's gubernatorial campaign. In a 1966 special election and the 1967 general election, he tried unsuccessfully to fill Sonny Montgomery's seat in the state Senate. In 1972, party leaders recruited him to run for the US Senate to keep James Meredith, the first Black student at Ole Miss, from getting the nomination by default. While President Richard Nixon heartily endorsed Thad Cochran and Trent Lott in their successful races for Congress, he ignored Carmichael to maintain favor with powerful Democratic senator James O. Eastland. However, Gil ran a surprisingly strong race against Big Jim. He became a new, refreshing face for the party. In 1974, he began listening to growing clamor for him to run for governor in 1975.

In his 2016 eulogy of Gil, the Reverend Canon David Johnson best described his lifetime friend's vision:

> Part of the reason that Gil was such a transformative person in our lives was that he was a visionary. He could peer over the horizon and see what was possible. . . . He was an anomaly in politics. He saw no barriers—racial, gender, social, or otherwise. He saw the raw human potential in individuals and in this state. . . . He cast off fear, bigotry, and classism. He sought unity rather than division. He embraced hope. He pointed toward the possibilities.

A conservative Scotsman by heritage, Gil envisioned a moral government playing a constructive role by providing citizens with good education, economic opportunity, and a fiscally responsible safety net for the poor and elderly. He also envisioned constrained government operating efficiently by rightsizing agencies to mitigate taxes and cull funds to provide for necessary programs. Gil called his approach, a modern form of constructive conservatism, "good government." His critics called it Gil's "blue sky" idealism.

Two key people helped him shape his approach. One was his political mentor, Gene Damon, a civil engineer in Meridian and another modern Republican Party pioneer. Gene believed strongly in efficient, effective government. He convinced Gil that applying his practical business experience to governing could eliminate waste, mismanagement, and corruption and allow funds to be prioritized to difference-making programs. Another influencer was Sidney Davis Jr., a Mendenhall banker. His research on a model constitution for Mississippi led Gil to believe that a new constitution would be the best vehicle to empower a governor to reorganize government and operate it more like a business. The final influence of his approach to governing came from Gil himself. A victim of the Great Flood of 1927 and a largely fatherless childhood, Gil was motivated to uplift Mississippi's disadvantaged through improved schools and better jobs. Gil ardently believed that this moral and constructive approach to governing would make a difference, lead to progress, and yield a better state for all Mississippians.

Gil met with me at his Volkswagen dealership in Meridian in late December 1974, following an introduction by David Johnson. "I remember the day in 1974 when he walked in and said that he had come to work for my gubernatorial campaign," Gil wrote in a 1996 letter to the editor for the *Meridian Star*. "When I said I had no money, he signed on as a volunteer." Well, almost a volunteer. In January 1975, I went to work as Gil's constant traveling aide for $100 a week. Later that year I served as press secretary for his campaign.

Gil anchored that campaign on how his businesslike, fiscally responsible vision of good government could move Mississippi ahead. Traveling daily with him, I came to marvel at its comprehensiveness—write a new, moral constitution to reorganize state government and strengthen executive power; run government like a business to eliminate waste, mismanagement, and corruption and utilize those efficiencies to make key programs effective; uplift the disadvantaged through improved schools and better jobs; build a competitive two-party system to produce better government policy; and diversify the Republican Party to pull people together.

Gil often praised former governor Hugh White, a successful businessman from his hometown of Columbia, for developing the Balance Agriculture with Industry (BAWI) program and taking other steps to advance Mississippi's economy. Gil also readily discussed controversial efficiency and effectiveness measures such as consolidating duplicative and eliminating wasteful state boards and agencies, reducing the number of counties, converting the elected Highway Commission into an appointed Transportation Commission to make it more comprehensive and professional, and changing the constitutional elected positions of secretary of state, attorney general, and state treasurer into appointed positions serving in the governor's cabinet. He regularly preached the benefits of a competitive two-party system.

And Gil tried to make his party more diverse and inclusive by recruiting Black Mississippians and reaching out to members of the NAACP. He attracted one surprising supporter, so surprising that the *New York Times* wrote about it: "Here, as in much of the South, Republicans have a country club image to most Black voters. Mr. Carmichael is working hard to overcome that, and he has recruited the only Black in the State Legislature, Robert Clark, a Democrat, to help him." In an oral history in the Mississippi Department of Archives and History, recorded by Jack Bass in 1992, Representative Clark explained why he supported Gil:

> And the ironic thing at that time [1975], you know, no statewide white candidate had ever in modern times asked any Black person for his or her vote publicly. They had not done it, and I made a vow that with all the investments I had in the development of Mississippi, . . . the next person that was elected governor was going to have to come out and have to make a public appeal for the Black vote. . . . And lo and behold Gil Carmichael agreed to do that.

Robert's willingness to break with his Black colleagues to support Gil's vision for Mississippi affirmed my confidence that Gil's approach would serve Mississippi well.

Gil lost that tough race to Cliff Finch in 1975. Many of us Carmichael insiders believed that was a turning point for the Republican Party. Had Gil won, he would have forever shifted the party's trajectory toward good government conservatism. Many of the bright young minds who supported William Winter in 1979 had supported Gil in 1975. They would have become prime targets for Republicans to recruit. Even die-hard Winter Democrats appreciated Gil's good government approach. For example, Dick Molpus, who worked for Winter and later became secretary of state, wrote me a letter in 1984 saying, "Many of the things we talked about in the Education Reform Act push [under Governor Winter] were issues that Gil talked about six years earlier." That same year Ray Mabus, another Winter staffer, who became state auditor (and later governor), wrote: "Gil Carmichael promoted some of the best ideas ever to come along in Mississippi politics."

I FIND MY VOICE

Although I was blessed with natural talent in math and science, writing became the preferred skill of my life. No doubt my obsession with novels played a role—as a child I read every volume of Tom Corbett and the Hardy Boys at the Canton Public Library.

In December 1965 I received late, and by then unexpected, word from Representative Arthur Winstead that I would be his last appointment to the United States Naval Academy. Two years there majoring in engineering honed my analytical skills in math and science. But an international relations class captured my interest. My professor connected me to the School of International Service at the American University. My Superintendent's List academic performance got me admitted. I transferred in the fall of 1967 with a National Defense Student Loan and a part-time job as a runner for Representative John Bell Williams. Soon, my interest in working on the Hill exceeded my interest in school, so I began working full-time as a legislative assistant for Representative Charlie Griffin, who had succeeded Williams. This whetted my interest in politics. Writing constituent letters and position papers also gave a start to my writing career. In 1970, a car wreck brought me home to Mississippi. Jack Shearer Jr., who served as Representative Griffin's administrative assistant, introduced me to Purser Hewitt, the editor of the *Clarion-Ledger* in Jackson. By May 1970, I was editing obituaries and working my way through Millsaps College. Not long afterward, Mr. Hewitt assigned me to cover the Mississippi Senate. Thus began my journalism career and early interest in state politics. Brief stops at the *Hattiesburg American*, Biloxi *Daily Herald*, *Meridian Star*, and Memphis *Commercial Appeal* followed. Then in 1975 I found my way into Gil's campaign for governor.

It was Gil who shaped my views on government and politics and motivated me to get involved in both. In 1976, newspaper entrepreneur and publisher John Emmerich gave me my political voice. He hired me as editor and publisher of the *Sun-Sentinel* weekly newspaper in Charleston, Mississippi. Amusingly, he somewhat regretted giving me that voice months later when I endorsed Gerald Ford for president over his choice, Jimmy Carter.

In 1977, I began writing a weekly political column entitled "Talking Politics" and distributing it to newspapers all over north Mississippi. A number of my columns from 1977 to 1979 informed north Mississippians about the good government approach offered by Gil and other constructive conservatives in the Republican Party. In November 1977, "GOP Goes after New Bedfellows" headlined my column that described party diversification efforts by Gil and Charles Pickering: "The main political activity is coming from the other side of the fence, the Mississippi Republican Party. Two Thursdays ago, State Republican Chairman Charles Pickering and GOP leader Gil Carmichael spoke to an NAACP gathering in Jackson. Their visit typifies the GOP commitment to include Blacks in the Mississippi party."

Chosen to finish a term on the GOP state executive committee from the Second Congressional District in 1977, I got to work closely with party chairman Pickering along with his new state party director, John Simms. That led in early 1978 to assisting in the preparation of the first Republican response to a Democratic governor's state-of-the-state address—Charles Pickering versus Governor Cliff Finch. I wrote about this.

PICKERING REFUTES FINCH IN HISTORIC RESPONSE

January 26, 1978

State Sen. Charles Pickering's broadside against Gov. Cliff Finch last week marks a new era in Mississippi politics. Never before has an opposition party responded to a governor's State of the State message with a counter message of its own.

Pickering, state chairman of the Mississippi Republican Party, took off his gloves and slapped Finch's platform up one side and down the other. "Full of obvious inaccuracies, misrepresentations and errors," Pickering said of the message. He called Finch's statement on Parchman [State Penitentiary] "simply not true."

Politics as usual, right? Well, it might have been. The clinker came when Pickering's response was mentioned in a forum of state legislators being interviewed on the ETV network. Those legislators, members of Finch's party, said Pickering hit the nail on the head—his statements and figures were accurate and Finch's weren't.

Pause a moment and let that sink in.

Many elected officials in Mississippi have often agreed with Republican statements and have in fact supported Republican candidates. It was always behind the scenes, though. But here were some actually speaking publicly and strongly in favor of the Republican position.

Of course, that's what a good two-party system does. It provides voters with alternatives. False or inaccurate statements don't go unchallenged but are put under a strong spotlight for all to see.

In the past, the people of Mississippi have had to depend on the press or wait for another campaign to roll around for actions like Finch's to be challenged. It's much healthier for the voters and for the press for an opposition party to come forward and do its duty.

The state GOP also seems on the verge of accomplishing something it has never done—fielding a Republican candidate to run for Congress from the First District.

A new face in the First District political scene, T. K. Moffett, was to reveal today that he will challenge incumbent Jamie Whitten as a Republican. Moffett, whose political philosophy should put him in the moderate section of the state GOP, thus becomes a much more serious contender for Whitten's post. GOP leaders are said to be serious about Moffett's challenge and will devote time and resources to his campaign.

On another front the GOP seems to have flopped. No major Republican figure has stepped forward to tackle Sen. James Eastland this year. Gil Carmichael and Rep. Thad Cochran seem to have faded out of the picture, and Pickering appears to be more interested in governor than senator.

As the GOP search broadens, under the direction of just-retired chairman Clarke Reed, a new name has popped up. Haley Barbour, a Yazoo City lawyer and the just-retired executive director of the state GOP, has been mentioned as a possible candidate.

Barbour, just thirty years old but perhaps the fieriest speechmaker in the party, would be a definite longshot. But longshots don't always miss in Mississippi.

Later that year I would volunteer and serve as an aide in Pickering's campaign for the US Senate. Charles also helped develop my views of government and politics. He preached a form of good government conservatism that retained its commitment to fiscal responsibility but was willing to address the need for charity and opportunity for the poor.

No surprise, I joined Gil again in his 1979 campaign for governor as his media director with the expectation he would win. However, after he supported Gerald Ford for president in 1976 over Ronald Reagan, the more conservative side of the GOP rose up and recruited Leon Bramlett to challenge him in a primary. While Gil won that bruising race, it left him weakened politically and financially. On the Democratic side, William Winter upset favorite Lieutenant Governor Evelyn Gandy and entered the general election with momentum. That was not the best matchup for Gil, as both he and Winter favored similar ideas for education, government reform, diversity, and human well-being. Following the loss to Winter, Gil became frustrated with the party. In 1983 he chose to run for lieutenant governor as an independent and lost badly.

Regrettably, Gil would never win statewide elective office. However, he did remain a popular Republican figure in Mississippi. And in 1989 President George H. W. Bush appointed him head of the Federal Railroad Administration. He spent the last decades of his public life as a champion for innovations in multimodal transportation and a GOP icon.

After the 1979 loss, my story evolved as I moved to Meridian and changed careers from journalism to banking. In 1980, Lynn Campbell, who had worked in the 1979 campaign, agreed to marry me (a very lucky day for me). I remained active in party politics campaigning for Ronald Reagan, serving as chairman of the Lauderdale County Republican Executive Committee, and promoting Gil's good government agenda.

DIVERSIFYING THE REPUBLICAN PARTY

When I was age five, we moved to 122½ East Center Street in Canton. An older Black man named Ed lived in a one-room wooden shack in the back lot between my house and Ed Melvin's house. Big Ed, as we called him, gave me a small wooden gun he had whittled. It became my favorite toy for a while. One day, Big Ed was gone, days later his shack. To where and why I never knew. But I have always remembered his kindness to me.

In 1978, as editor and publisher of the *Tunica Times-Democrat*, I wrote several columns about Republicans working to attract Black voters. That December, I wrote about Black turmoil within the Democratic Party and young Black leaders' flirtation with Republicans.

YOUNG BLACKS CHALLENGE ESTABLISHED LEADERSHIP

December 14, 1978

The turmoil surrounding Black politics in Mississippi goes far deeper than the controversy roused by Charles Evers's independent campaign for the US Senate.

The union of the Loyalist and Regular factions of the Democratic Party in 1976 behind Jimmy Carter was at best a paper coalition. For while one central party committee emerged, it was still us versus them when decision-making time came around. This tentative union could only last while no pressure was exerted upon it.

Charles Evers's decision to run as an independent candidate for the US Senate against Democratic nominee Maurice Dantin and Republican nominee Thad Cochran provided that unwanted pressure, and the paper tiger lost its growl.

But Charles Evers was simply the straw that broke the camel's back. For evolution within the Black political leadership of Mississippi was already pressuring for change.

Evers, Aaron Henry, and other acknowledged leaders of the Black community gained their positions during the civil rights turmoil of the 1960s. Theirs were the voices raging against injustice. They were there in the jails suffering. They led the marches in the face of the auxiliary police forces with their billy sticks and helmets.

And when the racial fighting dwindled, they cemented their leadership positions by continuing to push and shove here and there, mostly through court action, and speaking out for the poor Blacks of Mississippi.

National attention focused on Evers and Henry and the white liberals championing their cause, such as Hodding Carter and Pat Derian. The massive influx of federal money into programs for the poor indirectly contributed to raising the influence of Black leaders to a level substantially above their brethren. As this happened, the racist fears died down, and Black leadership settled into a status-quo stance. When the union of the Loyalist and Regular factions finally occurred, Henry and numerous other Blacks became full-fledged members of the establishment, a 180-degree shift from their initial positions.

During these two decades of change, many of the old-time civil rights fighters died or retired from the limelight. And, as in all social cycles, new blood began to appear in leadership circles. Most of the young blood flowed down the paths set down by the older blood. Henry, Evers, and others were viewed as heroes of the Black movement in Mississippi. And they could do no wrong.

Recent events have altered that view, however, and the young blood is overflowing the old pathways.

The young Turks decided not to go along with Henry's decisions to back former white racists such as retiring Sen. James O. Eastland. Others were itching to have their own voices heard instead of drowned out by Henry.

Examples of the latter group would be present executive director of the NAACP, Dr. Emmett Burns (Burns has developed a cordial relationship with the Republican Party and a special relationship with probable GOP gubernatorial candidate Gil Carmichael) and Skip Robinson (whose energizing of the United League in north Mississippi has supplanted the role formerly played by the NAACP).

Evers, ever aware of the political opportunities around him, saw the change going on and decided to capitalize on it this year. His race crystalized the frustration many young Black leaders have been feeling for a number of years.

Evers, however, is an old surfer riding the crest of a new wave. He is due for a fall, and other, younger faces will ride it far better.

Henry stayed in the boat and got swamped. Bill Minor reported last week that Henry may be toppled from his cochairmanship of the Democratic Party as young forces there try to strengthen the bonds between its various elements. Rumor circulating through the recent NAACP convention that Henry would be exiled from the presidency was false, but its existence was a signal of changes to come.

Fundamental to the turmoil in Black politics is the belief of young members that the strides made in Mississippi to overcome racism have not gone far enough. They feel Blacks have been admitted but haven't been allowed to join the mainstream. They point to the Democratic Party's failure to generate and support a major statewide Black candidate as evidence.

Thus "Black Christmas" boycotts and marches by the United League or local Black groups have reappeared during these times of mild racial tension.

At the heart of the matter is the undecided question of whether Blacks in Mississippi want to remain a cohesive minority or dissolve into a racist-free majority. The latter is the ideal, but the former fits the reality better. Up to this time Blacks have been unsuccessfully trying to do both.

Accompanying the column was a political cartoon I had a local artist draw that depicted a long line of Black field hands standing at an open door to a Delta plantation cocktail party. The caption read, "Would you like us to join your party?" After publication, a large white man with a gun strapped to his belt came in the office and let me know forcefully "we ain't having none of that" in Tunica County. The former owner of the paper had been coming in to write a weekly column but never came back after the man's visit. The artist said her husband told her not to draw any more cartoons.

A few years later as chairman of the Lauderdale County Republican Executive Committee, I worked to implement Gil's goal of diversifying the party, hoping to start moving beyond race-oriented politics. While successful in recruiting minority members to the county committee, I became frustrated by the lack of similar progress at the state level. In September 1981, my letter to Mike Retzer, the state party chairman, prompted him to aggressively encourage Black Mississippians to join the party. A confidential letter, it was fairly brutal in assessing the challenges facing the party. But it also suggested steps the party should enact to improve its image and attract Black voters.

Senator Thad Cochran wrote to me on October 6, 1981, saying, "I strongly support the recommendations you are making for expanding the appeal of the Mississippi Republican Party. I think we should move quickly to implement the changes you recommend."

My "confidential" letter ended up in the hands of a reporter for the Memphis *Commercial Appeal.* (Not by me, and I never learned by whom or why it was made public.) That resulted on November 10, 1981, in a bold headline spread across the top of the *Commercial Appeal*'s Tri-State section.

OFFICIAL URGES GOP TO CORRECT ITS "ANTI-BLACK" IMAGE

By Guy Reel

Commercial-Appeal (Memphis)

November 10, 1981

MERIDIAN, Miss.—A letter from a Republican Party county chairman to the statewide GOP chairman urges that the party correct its "serious image problems" among Blacks in an effort to wrest more Black votes from Democratic control.

Lauderdale County Chairman Bill Crawford says in the letter to Mississippi Republican Party Chairman Mike Retzer that Democratic politicians have damaged the GOP's image in the state by focusing on race.

"They [Democrats] merely have to point to our State Executive Committee as a 'lily-white' entity, our full-time staff's lack of any Black member, and campaigns such as Liles's [Williams, who lost a Fourth District congressional race to Democrat Wayne Dowdy earlier this year], which had no Black participation, to create a believable public image of the Republican Party as anti-Black," Crawford says in the four-page letter.

"Against this background, any policy statements made by Republicans that can be construed as anti-Black take on a much more caustic tone than is intended."

The September 17 letter, an intraparty communication that was not intended to be made public, outlines a possible Republican strategy to counter its eroded image in three areas—race, wealth, and negativism. It suggests that Republicans develop an effective media campaign to influence public opinion and that the party keep its distance from such "negative" groups as the Moral Majority and the National Conservative Political Action Committee.

"We've lost our momentum of a good image," Crawford said in an interview. "We used to be viewed as the underdogs in the state, as the good guys. Now we're viewed as the rich fat cats and as the bad guys. The fat cat image and the anti-Black image are bad labels for the overall party."

The GOP in Mississippi, until recently far outnumbered by the Democrats, has traditionally struggled to win elections and support. However, with the election of Sen. Thad Cochran and Rep. Trent Lott, both Republicans, and the party's victory in the 1980 presidential election, the Republicans have gained new strength.

But at least some of that strength has come from a source that many Republicans say they don't want. After the Democratic Party in 1976 reconciled a split between an all-white faction and a biracial faction of the party, some of those in the all-white faction defected to the GOP.

Black Republicans Wilbur Colom and Les Range said that if the trend continues, Blacks and whites could become polarized within the two-party system.

"I think it's possible," Range said. "But there's a group of Blacks who are going to be involved in the Republican Party come hell or high water. I think an effective way to change a party is by working from inside the structure."

Crawford's letter says the party should be aware that some perceive it to be anti-Black and that the GOP's problem is primarily one of image. His suggestions:

- Expand the Republican State Executive Committee from thirty to thirty-five or forty members. If five members are added, he says, four should be Black. If ten members are added, seven should be Black.
- Hire a Black full-time staff member. "This staff member should not be designated as the 'Black field man' but should be an integral part of the staff," Crawford says in the letter. "I suggest a Black person be hired to fill the press role on the staff. The first step in changing any image is to convey that change to the press. Hiring a Black person as press coordinator would convey the message loud and clear."
- Make a "sincere effort" to involve Blacks in district and statewide campaigns.
- Form a task force to develop policy statements and to communicate the party's philosophy to the Black community.
- Develop more Black candidates for office.
- Be more visible on college campuses in an effort to recruit young Blacks.

Colom said the suggestions, some of which were formed with his help, are worth pursuing. "You've got to narrow what you're doing to what you can realistically accomplish," Colom said. "Philosophically, we have to offer alternatives. Everyone can say what's wrong with the Great Society programs [of Lyndon Johnson], but the problem is we haven't come up with viable solutions. We have to work on the alternatives, and if we can't offer any, there's a deficiency in our way of thinking."

Crawford points out in the letter that the GOP's wealthy image has also hurt its potential in attracting new voters.

"References to [former senatorial and gubernatorial candidate Gil] Carmichael in 1979 as the 'millionaire' businessman and headlines like the one after Dowdy's win—'Dowdy Upsets Well-Heeled Williams'—illustrate the problem."

Carmichael said he also believes the party should work harder to get its message across. "Just about every person in the Black community that I've talked to has said their main desire is to have a job within the system," he said. "If we expect to carry any statewide race, any Republican candidate has got to get the message across to a decent percentage of Blacks."

Crawford tells Retzer in the letter that Republicans should answer the "fat cat" charges by going on the offensive. He suggests that the GOP should point out that their Democratic opponents are often just as wealthy as the Republicans. He says that nonwealthy Republicans should be recruited to participate in campaigns and that wealthy Republicans should be "deemphasized." The way to accomplish that, he said, is to communicate more effectively with the press.

Crawford then suggests that a public relations task force be developed to "disclose the true image of our party to both the media and the public. . . . Besides establishing give-and-take relationships, there should also be a well-thought-out image-building campaign."

Finally, Crawford focuses on what he calls the "negativism" given the Republican Party by such groups as the Moral Majority and the NCPAC.

"Liles's (Williams) campaign suffered because people saw (Ku Klux) Klan members actively campaigning for him," Crawford says. "Distance must be kept between campaigns and such groups."

Both Crawford and Colom emphasized that the letter was not intended to be made public. "Sometimes you'll say things privately that are true but wouldn't sound right in public," Crawford said.

Still, Republican leaders are more than willing to discuss the party's problems in attracting Black members.

"There's definitely a perception problem in the Black community about the Republican Party," said state GOP Executive Director Lanny Griffith. "I don't know whether that's a failure in our approach or a failure in our ability to communicate."

As for the possibility that the GOP Executive Committee may be expanded soon, Griffith said it would be the job of the task force to make recommendations.

"As long as we don't have quotas," he said—"that's one of those things that happens and that you have to watch when you're deliberately trying to adjust to a problem."

Despite his letter and an earlier one that he said was "more to the point," Crawford said he doesn't believe the Republican Party in the state is in any danger of becoming a single-race entity.

"I don't have a great fear of that," he said. "It's not going to be all white with a fundamental concept of racism. It's a healthy party that has been unable to attract the Black voter."

That, said Carmichael, is fundamental to the survival of the party in the future. "If we want to be in office," he said. "We'd better."

Despite Senator Cochran's support and the hoopla the article engendered, the party took no immediate action to change things. In the spring of 1983, Thad finally coaxed the state executive committee to expand from thirty to thirty-five members and add three minority members. The three were Eugene F. Young, a Meridian contractor whom I had helped recruit (his brother was Democratic state representative Charles Young); Samuel Coley, a retired postal worker from Columbus; and William Dease, manager of computer operations at Jackson State University. Still, this looked to be more tokenism than sincere welcoming.

In June 1983, the *NEW ERA* newsletter published by Black Republican pioneers Wilbur Colom, an attorney in Columbus, Les Range, a community development practitioner from Jackson, Carl Lee, a community activist from Columbus, and Chester Smith, a business developer from Greenville, printed a blistering article I wrote.

A TWO-BY-FOUR FOR MISSISSIPPI GOP

NEW ERA newsletter
June 1983

Do you know the difference between a mule and the Mississippi Republican Party?

If you wallop a mule between the eyes with a two-by-four, you'll get its attention.

Black voters have walloped the Mississippi GOP for years and still can't get the attention of the party's leadership. And they do carry a pretty big stick, what with 30% to 35% of the vote in most contested statewide races.

Poor and elderly white voters, especially those from rural areas, are ignored by the Mississippi GOP, too. Yet, these two voter groups together constitute a majority in Mississippi. Thus, it should be no wonder that no Mississippi Republican has captured a majority vote in a statewide election in over one hundred years.

Sen. Thad Cochran, the only Republican elected in a statewide race since Reconstruction, garnered 46% of the vote in a three-way race. Charles Pickering got 48% against Bill Allain in the 1979 attorney general's race. Gil Carmichael got over 47% in 1975 against Cliff Finch. These are the best-performing candidates the modern-day Republican Party has yet to offer to the Mississippi electorate. But none could capture a majority of the vote.

In 1980, Ronald Reagan's popularity was near a zenith in Mississippi. Yet Reagan received just 50.68% of the Mississippi vote, edging failure-ridden Jimmy Carter by a mere 11,808 votes.

Who, then, is so simple as to ask why the Mississippi Republican Party does not have a stable full of young candidates raring to run for statewide office? Even if the stables were full of qualified men and women, it's doubtful they would eagerly take on the task of running for statewide office. In fact, the stable is practically empty.

The Mississippi Republican Party leadership has done little to make the party palatable to Blacks, poor whites, and the elderly. Invariably, the party has taken stands contrary to the Black community. It shows very little concern for the problems facing the poor and the elderly. Rather, the party's leadership is more aroused by those issues important to the upper economic levels of white Mississippi society.

Nothing is more exemplary of where the heart of the party's leadership lies than its State Executive Committee. Until this spring, the committee was "lily-white." Sen. Cochran, in anticipation of his 1984 reelection campaign, stepped in and demanded that the committee be expanded to include Blacks. Now there are three on the thirty-five-member committee. There remains a general lack of representation of poor, rural whites. Alas, there is no adequate rebuttal to the Democratic cliché "country-club Republicans" when applied to this group.

Even worse, that is exactly the image it exudes. At least a pragmatic, sensible group of country clubbers would fashion an image attractive to major voter groups. Not so with this current group of Republican leaders. They were appalled at Cochran's move to include Blacks on the committee. They endorsed it only because of Cochran, not because they concluded it made any sense.

Such regressive and impractical leadership imparts no attractive, positive reason for any ambitious person to seek a Republican candidacy. On the contrary, it encourages the ambitious and able to shy away from the party.

Consider the trouble the Mississippi GOP had finding a candidate for governor this year. Leon Bramlett had been preparing to run for four years. When a tragedy in his family initially caused him to back out of the race, only veteran GOP candidate Gil

Carmichael showed any interest in the Republican nomination for governor. There was no enthusiasm at all for the moderate Carmichael among the GOP leadership. Many of them had helped recruit Bramlett to ambush Carmichael in 1979. As a result, Carmichael has left the party to pursue an independent candidacy. In the meantime, the party leadership sought far and wide for a gubernatorial candidate. No one responded to the search. It became apparent that the Republican gubernatorial nomination handed to you on a silver platter was not a very tempting morsel.

Luckily for the GOP, Bramlett's personal situation reached a status that allowed him once again to consider running. Since the party leadership had run off Carmichael, Bramlett was able to step back into the picture and claim he was doing so because no other Republican had stepped forward.

However, Bramlett's reemergence does not diminish the GOP's plight. There still is little appetite among candidates for the lesser statewide nominations the GOP has to hand out. In fact, there appear to be only two other statewide Republican candidates in 1983: State Rep. Jerry Gilbreath of Laurel and new Republican Roger Googe. Googe is seeking the attorney general's post and Gilbreath is seeking the secretary of state position. As a longtime Republican, he was pretty much stuck with the GOP label. But he has made it clear his candidacy will not mirror the party image, but will involve Blacks, labor, the poor, and other groups foreign to most Republican campaigns.

Gilbreath's candidacy reflects the fact there are those in the Republican ranks who understand that the GOP must reach out to a majority of the people if it ever hopes to be a major force tugging in that direction. Unfortunately, there are others pulling against him. And there is no strong leadership within the party hierarchy able or willing to force the action in the necessary direction.

Thus, not only are GOP candidates scarce in 1983, but there is nothing of consequence happening to remedy that situation in the near future. However, if walloping can get mules to eventually come around, there may still be hope for the Mississippi GOP.

(Bill Crawford is a bank executive and chairman of the Lauderdale County GOP.)

In the end, my two-by-four approach did not work any better than the aspirational method used by Gil and Charles Pickering. While Charles would go on to become a strong champion for racial reconciliation in

Mississippi and played a key role in ameliorating the Southern Baptist Convention's position on race, the party and its base would make no real inroads with Black voters. Republican candidates would mumble about attracting Black voters but would only poll 10 percent or so in statewide elections.

The party took a strong turn away from diversification during Kirk Fordice's terms as governor. "One likely effect of Fordice's outspoken conservatism was a stampede of white conservatives to the GOP," wrote Mississippi State University political scientists Stephen D. Shaffer and David Breaux in their 1997 treatise "Mississippi Politics in the 1990s: Ideology and Performance." Saying Fordice had "alienated African-Americans" by his conservative rhetoric, they noted, "[b]y 1994 fully 57% of white Mississippians now considered themselves Republicans, while only 29% remained Democratic."

In 2007 my friend C. D. Smith, the Black regional manager for AT&T in Meridian, ran as a Republican for House District 84. The district was constituted mostly of parts of Lauderdale and Clarke Counties, but also pieces of Newton and Jasper Counties. Among four candidates in the first primary, C. D. led with 45 percent of the vote. In the runoff he got 45 percent again but lost. The contest was marred by some candidates and their allies playing the race card. "We ain't having no [Black person] represent us" was a common refrain. In 2008, Governor Haley Barbour appointed C. D. to the Board of Trustees of the State Institutions of Higher Learning (the College Board).

My Republican Party would attract both successful and opportunistic Black members here and there—in 2023, Rodney Hall of Southaven was elected as the first Black Republican state representative since 1873—but did not transform into a diverse party, as Gil and other good government conservatives envisioned. Race-based politics would help hold Mississippi at the bottom.

A NEW, MORAL STATE CONSTITUTION

You know, "change" is one of those key political words. Everybody wants change. But not everybody wants the same changes. So smart politicians promise to "change things for the better" but seldom tell us what changes they're talking about. They even less often spell out the details of specific changes. Those candidates who do tell us, frequently do not win. Our own Gil Carmichael may be the best example of one who spelled out changes in too much detail to win.

Gil taught me that the essential problem with Mississippi government lay with its constitution. "The old 1890 constitution is what's keeping Mississippi on the bottom," he said, because it gave the legislative branch of government much greater authority than the executive branch, it thwarted long-range planning, it promoted a bulky, unmanageable judiciary, it had numerous antibusiness sections, it was too cumbersome, it was outdated, and it represented an age of bigotry and hatred. In his 1975 race, Gil believed that his Hugh White "run government like a business" argument could help him gain support for modernizing the state constitution, contending that the 1890 constitution kept Mississippi stuck at the bottom with low wages and a weak economy. While he did attract the support of many business leaders, he was unable to get many top Republicans to buy into this vision.

In April 1983, the *Clarion-Ledger* published an op-ed I wrote that was right out of Gil's good government playbook. It pointed out "sacred cows" that state leaders were reluctant to change and challenged the *Clarion-Ledger* to take them on.

SAYS OTHERS LACK BACKBONE, TOO

April 24, 1983

A newspaper with the presumption to name an entire Sunday section "Perspective" should see its way clear to incorporate the meaning of the word into its editorial process. But your March 9 editorial, "No Backbone: Legislators Scorn Responsibility," lacked perspective.

It fogged up a couple of other things, too.

Your argument, simply put, was that our spineless legislators preferred to deprive schoolchildren and the mentally handicapped of needed services as opposed to raising taxes during an election year. In so doing, you held out Gov. William Winter as the emblem of "backbonism."

Let me unfog one small thing before I tackle your perspective. Your editorial stated that the Budget Commission had submitted its hit list for more cuts, and that "[i]t doesn't take a genius to see what our ostrich-like legislators [were] doing. Schoolchildren and the mentally handicapped don't vote."

Whoa! Isn't the chairman of that nasty Budget Commission none other than Mr. Backbone, Gov. Winter? Lt. Gov. Brad Dye is also a member of the Budget Commission. Yet all your scorn was aimed at legislators. Perhaps there is a lack of backbone elsewhere, too.

Now, back to perspective. In the dim light of your editorial there were only two choices—the "evil" choice of cutting needed services and the "good" choice of raising taxes. How clear cut that appears! Turn up the light, though, and you might see things differently. You might, for instance, discover that once upon a time there was a William Winter who tried to convince his people that some jobs in state government were unnecessary and that significant constitutional revision was necessary for state government to function properly. That William Winter helped abolish the position of elected state tax collector after he filled the post for two highly profitable terms. But his fervor for significant constitutional revision faded. Could it have faded because his political ambitions came into conflict with what was good for the state? Shades of our pusillanimous legislators!

Had our current governor pursued constitutional revision, however, our current revenue picture might not be so dismal.

Let's face the truth. Mississippi's archaic governmental structure promotes waste, inefficiency, and corruption. It needs to be reorganized and streamlined from top to bottom.

You too readily accepted the premise that no tax increase means "crying needs" will have to be abandoned. Not so. Many sacred cows should be sacrificed before depriving the truly needy of assistance.

You too hastily limited your "no backbone" scorn to our legislators. They do not suffer that malaise alone. Add Gov. Winter. Add all the other executive branch elected officials who refuse to touch, much less sacrifice, the sacred cows that devour so much of our resources.

What sacred cows?

How about our system of county government? Too many counties have not "elected" the county unit system, thereby allowing duplication, waste, and corruption to continue unthwarted.

How about the multitude of statewide elected officials with separate offices, separate staffs, separate budgets, and separate agendas? Do we really need to separately elect a secretary of state, attorney general, state treasurer, commissioner of insurance, state auditor, and commissioner of agriculture and commerce?

Couldn't we better organize these positions under the office of governor and cut out much duplication and waste?

Wouldn't the same hold true for the State Highway Commission? How about the number of legislators? Is there no duplication or waste in having a Department of Agriculture and Commerce and a Department of Economic Development and a Cooperative Extension Service with all their subsidiary divisions working independently of each other? Has anyone evaluated the necessity of their services in view of difficult economic times?

Are all our agencies, boards, commissions, departments, bureaus, and councils and their attendant staffs really necessary? Has anyone yet discovered just how many of these entities there are?

Reducing such overlapping would require stepping on very powerful toes. It is much easier and politically wiser to raise taxes as Gov. Winter preferred or to cut services as the legislature preferred.

This is where backbone comes in, or should I say, "goes out."

These remarks are designed to explain the broader perspective surrounding the cost and performance of Mississippi government. The impetus for constitutional revision given by J. P. Coleman two decades ago and Gil Carmichael in 1975 has not dwindled. Rather, the deterioration of revenue sources vis-à-vis the escalating costs of government has added to that impetus. Yet constitutional change remains a political albatross for any candidate.

However, if the Clarion-Ledger would focus its editorial power on the subject, gains might be made—gains that would benefit us all more than higher taxes or reduced services.

(William S. Crawford of Meridian, a former political columnist, is now vice president and administrative officer of the Great Southern National Bank.)

That fall I sought elective office myself running on Gil's good government platform and won a three-way general election with 46 percent of the vote to Democrat George Neville's 40 percent and independent Jim "Peewee" Knowles's 14 percent. As the new District 83 representative from Lauderdale County, I joined five other Republicans in the House (Bobby Everett, Joel Netherland, Dick Hall, Ron Aldridge, and Dwayne Thomas) and two in the Senate (Malcolm Mabry and Con Maloney) in the Democrat-dominated state legislature.

March 1985 found me in the hometown of Representative Mike Mills (now a federal district judge) speaking about a new state constitution, repeating Gil's favorite arguments.

SPEECH TO THE ABERDEEN ROTARY CLUB

March 1985

My assigned topic today is "a new constitution." I'm going to get around to that, but if you'll bear with me, I want to tell you the prayer I used to open the House session last Wednesday: Father, as we attempt to lead our state forward, help us remember your lesson that the test of leadership is example, the guise of leadership is humility, and the heart of leadership is charity.

Leadership is something we ought to pray for in Mississippi. Take Mike Mills. Mike has the talent, the ability, the potential—if you will—to be a great leader. He's smart. People respect his opinions. He'll stand up for what's right. But I'll tell you here today that the system has already begun to wear down Mike Mills. I can see the growing frustration in his eyes, the beginning of weariness that comes from trying to lead when the system is against you. The system has chewed up and spit out too many potential leaders. I pray it won't get people like Mike. We need them too much.

This system has its roots in our state constitution. Or, should I say our present state constitution. Our constitution is no sacred document like our US constitution. This is our fourth constitution in Mississippi. The first was adopted in 1817 when statehood was granted. The second was adopted in 1832. The third was adopted in 1869. And the present one was adopted in 1890. By the way, none of these constitutions, not a single one, was ever voted on and approved by the people of Mississippi.

So, what's wrong with our constitution? Well, in simple terms, it gives the legislative branch of government much greater authority than the executive branch; it thwarts long-range planning; it promotes a bulky, unmanageable judiciary; it has numerous antibusiness sections; it's too cumbersome; and it's outdated.

But let's not take my word for it. I'm hardly a constitutional expert. Let's consider what others have had to say about it.

"Everyone regularly checks up on his automobile's motor and his home appliances. A careful businessman periodically has his plant machinery and equipment examined and serviced in order to render it fit for efficient operation. Yet, today, Mississippians are using a state constitution which was written fifty-nine years ago and has had only minor repairs. It went into effect on November 1, 1890. Its thirty-three amendments have in many respects served to increase the inadequacy of the constitution rather than to lessen it." This was written in 1950 by a fellow named William N. Ethridge Jr. Not many years later he rose to the position of chief justice of the Mississippi Supreme Court. Judge Ethridge's work *Modernizing Mississippi's Constitution* is the most substantive study of the 1890 constitution. He recommended dramatic changes in the old document, many of which have been incorporated into the model constitution many are promoting for our state.

Among the more radical of Judge Ethridge's recommendations not included in the model constitution were to have a unicameral legislature and to abolish the post of lieutenant governor.

Before moving on, let me cite two other quotes from Judge Ethridge's work: "The federal Constitution vests in the President all of the executive power of the United States. But Section 116 of the Mississippi Constitution indicates that the Governor of Mississippi is not the custodian of all the power of the executive department. . . . [H]is powers are not commensurate with his responsibilities. . . . As one writer has said, the Governor is more of a 'chief observer' than a chief executive.

"Our legal [system] . . . follows no particularly logical pattern, and accordingly its unsystematic confusion results in friction, unnecessary expense, waste of time of litigants, and needless delay in the adjudication of controversies." Judge Ethridge made a strong argument for combining the circuit and chancery courts into one and for appointing all judges.

This is my favorite quote on the 1890 constitution, by J. P. Coleman, in his historic work *The Origin of the Constitution of 1890*: "The crying need of 1957 is for more confidence in ourselves and for less faith in the deluded idea that, by some magic or another, we of Mississippi can outrace a jet plane with an ox-cart." Judge Coleman, as you all know, led the fight in the late 1950s to revise the constitution. Interestingly, he may get that chance thirty years later.

Here's another sort of comment: "We have consulted our state's four living former governors, the Honorable J. P. Coleman, the Honorable Ross R. Barnett, the Honorable Paul B. Johnson Jr., and the Honorable John Bell Williams as leaders in the field of state government qualified by their dedicated public service to evaluate the need for constitutional reform; and we are authorized to express their unanimous opinion that there is an urgent need for modernizing our Constitution and increasing the efficiency of state government." This came from the Mississippi Economic Council in its 1975 publication Mississippi's Constitution: The Need for Change.

Another fellow spoke out strong in 1975 about a new constitution and has continued to do so through the present. My good friend Gil Carmichael believes that "the old 1890 constitution is what's keeping Mississippi on the bottom" because of its antibusiness provisions and its severe restrictions on long-range planning and program implementation by the executive branch of government.

It might interest you to know that a poll taken September 14, 1975, by a nationally recognized polling firm showed 65 percent of Mississippians favored a new constitution, 13 percent did not, and 22 percent were undecided; 64 percent favored gubernatorial succession with 16 percent disagreeing, and 10 percent undecided.

Now, I spoke of leadership earlier. I have been quoting some of yesterday's leaders. We have a number of new, energetic leaders trying to push our state forward today. Let me tell you what they have to say about a new constitution.

"Why has Mississippi been deficient in its quest for economic progress? I believe the answer is fundamental. . . . We have failed to assert leadership. We have seen that failure of leadership manifested not only in the personalities of our leaders but also in a structure of state government that restricts, retards, and inhibits the exercise of leadership. Mississippi's state government is an antiquated organizational structure that defies the development of an agenda for action, that stifles policy coordination, and that makes long-range planning nonexistent." Strong words by our very able state treasurer, Bill Cole.

"The governor of this state has no way to carry out long-range plans and long-range goals. . . . Forty-six other states have recognized that limitation and allow the governor, if he can be reelected, to serve more than one term. As someone who has been there as an aide, let me tell you—the last year of a governor's term, he is at his best—his influence, however, is at its worst. . . . In addition, thirty-five states have a formal cabinet. This governor, of course, does not have one. With staggered boards and no cabinet, the governor is like a president of a company who can't hire his vice presidents—his implementers of policy are not accountable to him. . . . Our problems in this state are historic and deep rooted. It will take long-range leadership to affect them." Our very highly regarded secretary of state, Dick Molpus, said this.

"I believe that one of the main obstacles to Mississippi achieving its potential has been its outmoded and inefficient constitution. Before Mississippi can truly move, we need a new constitution." Said by a man already making dramatic improvements in the way Mississippi government works, State Auditor Ray Mabus.

Cole, Molpus, and Mabus are fresh, new leaders in Mississippi government. It's very interesting to hear them speaking so forcefully about such an old and controversial issue.

Of course, the most important comment to come forward lately concerning a new constitution came from Governor Bill Allain last December. That's when he appointed Judge Coleman as chairman of a special committee to study the state constitution. It's my understanding that Judge Coleman plans to take charge of this committee and that the governor will complete his appointments soon after the legislature adjourns. Thus, Judge Coleman will be afforded a rare second chance to get his constitutional revision plan enacted.

Before closing, let me mention again the model constitution. This is a compilation of constitutional changes recommended from Judge Ethridge's time to the present. Sid Davis Jr., a Mendenhall banker and past president of the Leadership Mississippi Alumni Association, has put these recommendations together into an actual document. Among the dramatic changes proposed in the model are these: (1) the executive branch would be strengthened by allowing gubernatorial succession, all other executive positions would be appointed by the governor, administrative agencies would be limited in number to twenty, and the governor would prepare the budget; (2) terms for legislative members would be changed to two years for House members and six years for senators, the number of legislators would be reduced, a majority of legislators could convene a special session, and constitutional rules governing legislative actions would be repealed; (3) a unified judicial system would be established with the governor making appointments, a retirement age for judges would be established, and judicial terms would last seven years; and (4) constitutional restrictions on corporations and other antibusiness provisions would be repealed.

Political columnist Wayne Weidie is convinced a new constitution will never come about because the issue is too complicated and not "sexy" enough for the average voter. But I think something Dan Davis wrote in an August column in the [Aberdeen] Examiner may be more telling. I suspect constitutional change is going to come about because, as Dan said, "[i]t doesn't look like the issue is going to go away."

I pray it doesn't go away, so our future leaders, like Mike Mills, will have the tools needed to make the system work for the people of Mississippi, not against them. Thank you.

At the urging of Cole, Molpus, and Mabus, Governor Bill Allain in 1985 appointed a 350-member study committee led by former governor J. P. Coleman to look into the need for a comprehensive rewrite of the state constitution. I served on the education subcommittee. The committee issued a report with 150 change recommendations. A number of us legislators championed a bill to pursue those recommendations in a constitutional convention. It passed the Senate, but we could not get it to the floor in the House. Two key recommendations did survive. In 1986, the legislature passed and voters approved a concurrent resolution to amend the constitution to allow gubernatorial succession, a key change Gil thought vital to a governor's powers. In 1992, the legislature passed and voters approved a ballot initiative process to amend the constitution (upended on a technicality in 2021 by the Mississippi Supreme Court).

When he campaigned for governor in 1987, Ray Mabus said he would push for a new constitution. But after he took office in 1988, that effort never materialized. Neither did efforts by Cole and Molpus gain any traction. And no Republicans stepped up. Gil was the last major Republican leader to advocate for a new constitution.

As a last hurrah, Gil in 1998 made a series of speeches calling for a new constitution. No actions resulted. Mississippi's chaotic administrative structure, the enabler of so many holes in the whole, remained in place.

GOVERNMENT REORGANIZATION

While serving as a member of the legislature and as chairman of the Lauderdale County Council of Governments, I initiated a successful effort to combine the city and county tax collection departments. The legislature's Performance Evaluation and Expenditure Review (PEER) Committee conducted a study to see if the merger would save money and improve services. It did, and we pushed through the merger. Later, as chairman of the Lauderdale Economic Development Authority, I helped lead a successful effort to combine the chamber of commerce, tourism agency, and economic development authority into one organization. While not easy, reorganizing government at the local level proved more doable than at the state level.

Many governors and most citizens see government as a public business financed by taxpayer dollars that should be well managed. But Mississippi history shows that our state government more resembles kudzu—the "vine that ate the South." A little bit of kudzu can grow up to a lot before you know it. Pruning has little impact. Kill a section and it reappears. For successful long-term control of kudzu, experts say, it is necessary to use some method to kill or remove the kudzu root crown and all rooting runners.

Every government program in Mississippi has had its own "root crown"—a powerful legislator, official, or interest group—with "rooting runners." Take on the "W" and you take on the alumnae (as I learned the hard way); the Cooperative Extension Service and you take on the county agents and their friendly farmers, foresters, tomato growers, and quilters; Medicaid and you take on the poor, nursing homes, children of nursing home clients, and the medical community; highways and you take on road builders, local officials, and economic developers; tax breaks and incentives and you take on the business community; schools and you take on parents, teachers, and their formidable allies. Rooting beneficiaries everywhere!

Historic efforts to rein in runaway government accomplished little. In 1932, the Institute for Government Research of the Brookings Institution studied Mississippi government. Its *Report on a Survey of the Organization and Administration of State and County Government in Mississippi* recommended a maximum of twelve agencies. A study by Robert Highsaw and Carl Mullican, *The Growth of State Administration in Mississippi*, suggested seventeen agencies in 1950. A group of CEOs said thirty-two agencies in 1971. These thoughtful recommendations got nowhere with the Mississippi legislature, which wielded the power over agency creation and dissolution. In 1817 the state started with eight administrative agencies, by 1932 there were eighty, by 1950 just over one hundred, and in 2023 over 140.

Gil Carmichael wanted government to be efficient and effective, organized and competent to frugally solve difficult problems, and able to work for the good of all Mississippians. He knew that would require reorganizing and rightsizing government to give the governor and executive branch more sway. He saw a new constitution as the best means to that end. But without that, he knew much could be accomplished if the Republican Party pushed his constructive vision of good government. As a young, energetic Republican leader, I was determined to be one of those pushers. When I joined those five other Republicans in the House in 1984, I got fully engaged in government reorganization efforts. In 1955, the legislature created the Commission on Budget and Accounting with the governor as chair but dominated by legislators. Then in 1983, due to Attorney General Bill Allain's separation of powers lawsuit, the governor was booted off the commission, and it was revamped into the Joint Legislative Budget Committee, totally controlled by legislators.

Elected governor, Allain had to realign key state budget players via a "government reorganization" bill. Representative Charlie Williams included me on the House task force working with Allain on the

Administrative Reorganization Act of 1984. This was my opportunity to push Gil's "efficient and effective" approach. Sid Salter highlighted this in a 1984 column entitled "Views of a Journalist Who Turned Legislator." He wrote, "Even as a Republican freshman in a Democratic House, Crawford has been hailed as a prime mover-and-shaker on the governmental reorganization that was finally hammered out during the waning days of the session. Colleagues in the House say the Meridian legislator gained some respect in the chamber for his gutty floor performance." Sid's description was a little over the top—well, a lot over. My contributions to the reorganization bill, besides speaking for it, were to require the governor to submit a balanced budget proposal to the legislature annually and to give the governor as much executive power as possible, especially over the new Fiscal Management Board. Altogether, though, the act became more about government realignment than government reorganization. Allain's actions as attorney general and governor expanded the hole that government reorganization was intended to close.

The birth of my two children and major promotions at the Great Southern National Bank left me little time for a demanding, though fulfilling, part-time job in the legislature. My time as an elected public official pushing Gil's good government approach ended, but I could still write, hold other important positions, and stay engaged with politics. My writing, however, for a while became focused on bank reports and regulatory communications with only limited op-ed pieces for the *Meridian Star* and the *Clarion-Ledger*.

During my time in the legislature, state Republican leaders had begun to move away from Gil's good government approach. In particular, to recruit county supervisors to switch parties, they took a soft line on corruption to contrast with Democratic State Auditor Ray Mabus. In an initiative later to be dubbed Operation Pretense, Mabus had brought in federal investigators to bust up longtime supervisor corruption. Since my allegiance was more to Gil's good government approach to governing than to the party itself, my ties to the Republican Party began to fray. During the 1987 gubernatorial campaign, I listened for the candidate most likely to stick with Gil's approach. I did not know GOP nominee Jack Reed and was disheartened when he seemed to align with the party leadership's approach to supervisor corruption. The candidate that sounded most like Republican Gil Carmichael to me was Democratic nominee Ray Mabus. He campaigned for governor as an anticorruption champion who would focus on reorganizing and streamlining state government. I resigned from the Republican Party in order to vote in the Democratic primary and publicly supported Mabus, hoping he would succeed in these areas where others had failed. He did not. His major government reorganization proposals failed to pass the legislature. His successes were limited to closing charity hospitals, enacting county unit system legislation, and replacing the Fiscal Management Board with the Department of Finance and Administration.

In hindsight, Jack Reed might have been the one who could and would have accomplished much of Gil's good government approach. Later I would get to know him and learn of his extraordinarily constructive leadership in Tupelo and northeast Mississippi.

Beginning in 1989 and thereafter I would support numerous Republican candidates but did not get back involved in party activities. One of those candidates in 1991 became the first Republican governor elected since Reconstruction—Kirk Fordice. A successful businessman like his friend Gil Carmichael, Kirk pursued a conservative, businesslike approach to make government more efficient. Soon after he took office, I wrote the following letter to the editor about that. It was published in the *Clarion-Ledger* in March 1992.

GOVERNOR FORDICE WILL REINSTATE "REALITY" INTO GOVERNMENT

March 13, 1992

A decade ago, your newspaper dared to challenge our institutions of government to do better, to become more efficient to eliminate waste and duplication. A little over four years ago, you joined with many of us in promoting one Ray Mabus, who favored reforming and streamlining government, ending waste and duplication, etc.

How ironic that today you castigate Gov. Kirk Fordice for finally moving to accomplish these things.

But, wait, his ways aren't the correct ways. Yes, it's one thing to assail the sacred cows of Jim Buck Ross's agriculture empire and corrupt, inefficient county government, but quite another to challenge education and human services.

How ironic that the institutions most in need of improvement, i.e., reform, are held unassailable by the champions of reform.

Oh, but Gov. Fordice's attitude isn't "politically correct." He's frustrated with the never-ending public demands for extra-special treatment by minorities. He promotes religious activists to key positions. He says outrageous things.

How ironic that these traits mirror so much of Mississippi.

As an iron-handed representative of Mississippi's frustrated and overburdened taxpayers, Kirk Fordice is positioned to do more good for Mississippi than any governor since Hugh White.

My former colleagues in the media too often allow rhetoric and good intentions to temper reality. Reality in the business world is having to make payrolls, meet production deadlines, satisfy customers, and adequately reward stockholders. Reality requires efficiency, service quality, and innovation.

My former colleagues in the legislature too seldom allow reality to temper their rhetoric and good intentions. With an open purse from taxpayers, government has no impetus to retool, streamline, or change products. Thus, reality in the world of government comes only via crisis and taxpayer revolt. Mississippi taxpayers elected Kirk Fordice to close the purse and bring business reality into government.

One of two positive results will come from the Fordice years. One, he will upend government and challenge its institutions to improve. Or, two, he will upend government, challenge its institutions to improve, then guide an efficient, frugal Mississippi into the new century. The first is his destiny, the second his opportunity. Either way, Mississippi benefits. Just as pain leads to pleasure and chaos to order, frugality in government leads to better government.

So long as Gov. Fordice keeps to his iron-handed ways and avoids the glad-handing environment of traditional politics, he will make a real difference . . . the sort of difference you once hailed.

How ironic.

The legislature continued to lack the smarts and political will to prioritize spending and eliminate nonessential and duplicative programs. As a result, Kirk could not get his proposals to streamline government passed. He did successfully implement the Budget Reform Act of 1992, which created the state's rainy day fund to help lessen the impact of future budget cuts.

Haley Barbour would become Mississippi Republicans' only good government conservative to serve as governor. A pragmatic, commonsense, fiscal conservative who understood that state government must serve all the people for the whole state to prosper, Haley faced significant budget shortfalls during most of his two terms as governor. He cut budgets and in 2009 reluctantly agreed to raise the cigarette tax to balance the state budget. He fought to rightsize government but also found ways to improve funding for education and economic opportunity.

When Haley took office in 2004, the Mississippi Economic Council (MEC) in coordination with university researchers had just completed Mississippi's most comprehensive and aggressive strategic planning process. Chaired by Ole Miss chancellor Robert Khayat, the rigorous, broad-based Blueprint Mississippi planning process spanned 2002 through 2003 and resulted in fifty-three key strategies with eleven recommended for immediate action. The eleven included lifelong learning, expanded pre-K and middle school programs, and teacher recruitment along with economic development and business goals. Barbour endorsed Blueprint and immediately incorporated four top goals into his own Momentum Mississippi initiative:

(1) Enhanced competitiveness and an improved business climate as a result of comprehensive tort reform, improved economic development incentives including new ones for existing businesses, and a public-private targeted industry recruitment program;

(2) Improved worker training through the streamlining of the workforce development system to a single Workforce Investment Board with training provided by the Mississippi Community and Junior College System and through increased training funds provided by

Unemployment Insurance Trust Fund transfers to the new Workforce Enhancement Training Fund;

(3) Improved technology transfer by creation of a private sector Angel Fund operated by the Mississippi Technology Alliance and ramping up university research and development; and

(4) Improved education by piloting early childhood development programs, initiating a strong, statewide dropout prevention program, and implementing alternative teacher certification programs.

Haley was able to achieve most of the four goals in his Momentum initiative. However, budget shortfalls and Hurricane Katrina devastation in 2005 hindered most Blueprint initiatives.

I was honored to serve in the Barbour administration as deputy director of the Mississippi Development Authority, a position I retired from in 2008. In 2009, I began writing weekly newspaper columns again.

Facing new budget shortages toward the end of his second term, Haley sought to utilize government reorganization to rightsize government by eliminating agency and program duplication. In his fall 2009 budget recommendation to the legislature, he included eighteen commonsense proposals to close, move, merge, and defund agencies and institutions—including merging universities and school districts. His pitch often sounded as controversial as Gil's: "There is no reason for each of the fifteen community and junior colleges to have its own 'back room' operation, such as payroll, insurance, and purchasing"; "A single such administration operation should be set up, preferably combined with the same functions for IHL universities. 'Shared services' saves money."

How many of Haley's eighteen proposals did the 2010 legislature embrace? I wrote about the answer.

BOLD STEPS NOT TAKEN

April 22, 2010

Back in November, facing multiyear budget cuts, Governor Haley Barbour proposed bold steps to reorganize and rightsize Mississippi government. Among them were eighteen proposals to close, move, merge, and defund agencies and institutions.

The legislature reconvened this week to finalize appropriations for next year. Guess how many of the eighteen proposals they embraced? None . . . despite $500 million in cuts this year, and more looming.

No university mergers—the legislature ignored the governor's call to merge Alcorn and Valley into JSU and MUW into MSU.

Still pending is the blue-ribbon commission report on K-12 consolidation. Due April 1, the report will likely come after the legislature adjourns. Ironically, College Board member Aubrey Patterson heads the commission. The College Board also disregarded the governor's university merger plans. Wonder what position Patterson will take on schools?

The Mississippi School for the Arts will not merge with the School for Math and Science. The School for the Deaf and Blind will not be moved. And no community college athletic programs or satellite campuses will be downsized or eliminated.

The legislature still has to cut up to $100 million more from next year's budget. That's on top of this year's $500 million.

None of the four mental health facilities or six crisis centers targeted by the governor will be closed.

No agencies will be consolidated or defunded as the governor recommended. The Mississippi Forestry Commission, the Department of Agriculture and Commerce, and related boards and commissions will not be consolidated. The Department of Banking and Consumer Finance will not be absorbed by the secretary of state. Grand Gulf Military Monument operations will not be taken over by the Department of Archives and History. And the Mississippi Technology Alliance, the Commission on the Status of Women, the Enterprise for Innovative Geospatial Solutions, and the Mississippi River Parkway Commission will not lose state funding.

ABC wine functions will not be privatized. The MDOT Enforcement Division will not move under the Department of Public Safety.

About $400 million in federal stimulus money propping up next year's budget will disappear on July 1, 2011.

Two meek steps: The governor recommended closing Oakley Training Center and merging MUW. Instead, the legislature is downsizing Oakley, and MUW is transferring its back-shop operations to MSU.

Periodically, most of us have to reorganize and rightsize our closets—push stuff we wear to the front; throw out stuff that doesn't fit any more. State government's closet is full of stuff that no longer fits our needs and some stuff that should be pushed to the front.

Sure seems like the right time for legislators to redo the state closet. Wonder if A&E's *Hoarders* might do a reality special on state closets?

When Haley appointed his Commission on Educational Structure to look into school district consolidation, his message to chairman Aubrey Patterson and other members called for a reduction of the 152 school districts by one-third. I wrote about that failure, too.

SCHOOL CONSOLIDATION DEAD ALREADY

September 16, 2010

Sigh.

The governor's Commission on Educational Structure can at long last rest in peace . . . like its soon-to-be-dormant recommendations.

Remember, this is the commission appointed by Governor Haley Barbour to show how to consolidate up to fifty school districts and save millions of taxpayer dollars.

Friday, September 10, it handed in recommendations that were due April 1. Guess that due date should have clued us.

No school districts were recommended for closure.

No savings were calculated.

Pummeled by those who oppose any form of consolidation, the nineteen commissioners ignored several bold options to consolidate school districts. Rather, they chose to meekly propose for the legislature to offer incentives for school districts to "voluntarily consolidate."

Closing one hand and most of the other, use your remaining fingers to count the number of voluntary consolidations in Mississippi over the past two decades. Yep, you've got fingers left over and a good indication of the likelihood of voluntary consolidation.

Give most commission members credit. A majority did approve a recommendation to force consolidation of "support services and back-office operations" in counties with multiple school districts.

Buried in the report's appendices you can find a chart showing the percentage of education money spent by category. Mississippi spends a higher percentage than most southern states for administration and operations. For example, Mississippi spends 3.1% of funds on General Administration while South Carolina spends 1.3%. Mississippi spends 12% on Operation and Maintenance while Tennessee spends 9.8%. This shows savings can be had.

Unfortunately, this one bold recommendation will be dead on arrival in the legislature.

While most of the nineteen commissioners favored this recommendation, among five who did not were Rep. Cecil Brown of Jackson and Sen. Videt Carmichael of Meridian. Since Cecil and Videt chair the House and Senate Education Committees that would get the proposed legislation, you can expect it to lie dormant if not die quickly. No doubt Cecil and Videt were influenced by State Superintendent Tom Burnham and his predecessor, IHL Commissioner Hank Bounds, who voted against the proposal. I also doubt they were encouraged by the Hinds County and Lauderdale County superintendents, who have no fervent desire to work closely with their city brethren and vice versa.

On another note, the commission report makes it clear that members had concerns about forcing consolidation on parents and taxpayers. Yet, they proposed no recommendation to give motivated parents or taxpayers a way to call for district or back-shop consolidation.

Folks, banks, businesses, and even the federal government know from experience that consolidation of administrative and operations functions can reduce costs. Given our dire state finances, you'd think opportunities like this would become priorities.

When he made his bold proposals, Haley had become one of the most powerful governors in Mississippi history, able to wield the limited powers of his office to get major proposals through the legislature and respond effectively to Hurricane Katrina. Yet, even mighty Haley could not get the legislature to rightsize government. Again, legislators could not find the will to prioritize spending, eliminate nonessential and duplicative agencies, or consolidate school districts. This despite Haley having to order huge cuts to balance the budget. He repeated efforts to rightsize government during his last year in office, but to no avail.

Years later the legislature would move on two of Haley's proposals. In 2014, six school districts were merged and two dissolved, but not the fifty that Haley wanted. In 2021, the MDOT Enforcement Division was moved under the Department of Public Safety.

STARVE THE BEAST

Over the years, one thing I have chronicled has been the goal of efficient government I learned from Gene Damon and Gil Carmichael (and tried to implement as a Kirk Fordice appointee and Haley Barbour deputy) falling out of favor with Republicans. In its place, the new breed of Republican leaders substituted antigovernment, antitax, starve-the-beast policies.

Haley Barbour's election spurred a wholesale shift in power from the Democratic Party to the Republican Party. However, as Republicans took control of state government, the rightsizing elements of good government that Gil promoted and Haley pursued fell out of favor. Governor Phil Bryant started the move toward Republican leaders' new approach. In 2012 he proposed squeezing budgets rather than taking constructive steps to rightsize state government. By 2016, Republicans' new "starve-the-beast" approach was in full swing.

(During this time, the tenor of my columns also changed. Phil called C. D. Smith, chairman of the nonprofit I ran, to complain. C. D. said he told the governor my columns had nothing to do with the nonprofit and were "always fact based.")

Economist Milton Friedman wrote about the concept that became known as "starve the beast" beginning in late 1960s. He said he was influenced by C. Northcote Parkinson's Second Law—"expenditure rises to meet income." Friedman and others argued that if government income was limited, expenditures would be limited, too. Their goal was to make government smaller, spend less, tax less, yet still function effectively. Significantly, their approach was to eliminate waste and nonessential programs to reduce expenditures, not cut spending willy-nilly. Ronald Reagan was one of the first Republicans to preach this approach.

Beginning with Governor Bryant's administration, leaders in the GOP-controlled legislature, influenced more and more by the populist antitax, antigovernment Tea Party, adopted their twisted version of "starve the beast." They sought to cut taxes first, then make government fit. They did this not by cutting waste, nonessential programs, or corruption but by implementing across-the-board spending cuts. Unlike the good government rightsizing approach, this approach cut the good along with the bad, harming important and essential programs. I wrote about "starve-the-beast" budgeting.

REPUBLICANS STRUGGLE TO FIND SMART WAY TO BUDGET

July 19, 2016

"Starving the beast" is a popular conservative approach to governance.

"If they [legislators] don't have the money, they can't spend it," one Republican operative explained, strongly endorsing this approach.

True enough, but as another longtime Mississippi leader told me, "'Starve the beast' is not a smart way to govern; in fact, it isn't governing at all."

Also true.

Supposedly, Republicans in charge of state government are seriously pursuing a smart way to govern. No, not the "working groups" announced by legislative leaders last week. The long-awaited performance-based budgeting and management system, first announced by the legislature in 1994, would identify wasteful and ineffective programs whose funding could be reallocated to programs that evidence says work. In other words, it would allow legislators to make smart, evidence-based budget decisions.

But, not yet.

Three and a half years ago, Lt. Gov. Tate Reeves and Mississippi House Speaker Philip Gunn created a partnership with the Pew Charitable Trusts and the John D. and Catherine T. MacArthur Foundation to develop an analytical system to support performance-based budgeting. The legislature's Performance Evaluation and Expenditure Review (PEER) Committee was assigned tasks to develop a state strategic plan, a comprehensive inventory of programs and costs, and performance measures and targets. The PEER Committee was to gather data to assess program performance. The Pew-MacArthur model was to calculate cost-benefit ratios for assessed programs.

Last year, the PEER Committee produced a comprehensive guide to 'splain performance-based budgeting to legislators. It included interesting results from a pilot application of the new model.

Unfortunately, it also showed that this smarter budgeting approach remains many years away from fruition. That leaves us with "starve the beast."

The problem with this approach is that it starves important and essential programs.

Thus, deferred repairs to roads and bridges will continue to reach crisis status while hundreds of millions of dollars go for nonurgent building projects and tax cuts. The Department of Health will eliminate clinics and maternity services and the Department of Mental Health psychiatric beds and addiction units while less important and nonessential programs continue to operate. And so on.

As one of my more conservative friends commented, "Roads and bridges are wonderfully simple examples, but there are so many other areas that need to be functional."

Quite frankly, the first thing that needs to become functional is the legislature's basic budget process. Turned murky and complicated by the horribly misnamed "Budget Transparency and Simplification Act," the budget process this past session featured pretend appropriations bills that were rammed through by leadership to get the bills past deadlines and into six-man conference committees. Leadership then allowed these committees to meet in secret, contrary to the rules. To cap it off, the committee-approved bills with real numbers were not given to members until the last minute, providing them with little opportunity for review or rebuttal.

Not a smart way to govern. Nor is starving the beast.

It's possible the legislature's new working groups could turn things around. But, in Mississippi, politics trumps smart nearly every time.

The budget mechanisms developed with the Pew Trusts to identify wasteful and ineffective programs remained, but the legislature did not use the process as envisioned. In 2017, Lieutenant Governor Tate Reeves and House Speaker Philip Gunn touted their great success in holding down the cost of government. But these results did not come from reducing funds for wasteful and ineffective programs; they came from "starving the beast" by holding down spending for nearly everything.

In 2017, Vicksburg columnist Charlie Mitchell observed, "Mississippi now leads the nation in the 'starve-the-beast' approach to governance with Lt. Gov. Tate Reeves as champion of the movement." When he succeeded Phil Bryant as governor, Reeves continued the "starve-the-beast" approach he had championed as lieutenant governor but with added emphasis on tax cuts. I addressed spending cut opportunities in a 2017 column.

CONTROLLING STATE SPENDING

May 4, 2017

One of my many anonymous critics on the Jackson Jambalaya blog zapped me last week over my column "A Peek behind Legislative Leaders' Rhetoric." In particular, he/she said I lack "a coherent alternate plan" of my own.

Well, I never guessed it might be a columnist's job to propose a whole budget plan. But, an avid reader could find elements of such a plan already published. Let's take a peek.

Last month I suggested rightsizing the legislature by cutting it in half. That step alone would signify legislators are serious about cutting nonessential programs.

In February I wrote about rightsizing universities. By raising admission standards, moving all remediation to community colleges, and eliminating subsidies for out-of-state tuition, enrollment would fall, thereby reducing IHL's need for more state funding, higher tuition, and more bond money. Previously I supported consolidating university back-office and administrative functions.

Back in 2010, I wrote, "There are no operating or financial reasons for eight universities and fifteen community colleges—or 142 state agencies, 152 school districts, 82 counties, and 200 plus municipalities for that matter—to maintain separate back-room operations." Since, I have written favorably about limiting school districts to one per county, thereby consolidating financial, administrative, transportation, and other nonclassroom services to reduce costs.

I agreed with Governors Phil Bryant and Haley Barbour on their proposals to allow state agencies exemptions from personnel regulations to rightsize their workforces. I supported Barbour's calls to consolidate school districts and to reduce tax-dollar support for school athletics and community college sports.

I have written numerous times about the excessive costs of our broken PERS system. Charging employers 15.75 percent of wages is exorbitant. That's at least $350 million too much per year, most of it coming from state funds. Reducing this burden on taxpayers should be a priority.

There's more, but maybe you and my critic can sense what I think a coherent spending plan should include.

The key is this—to effectively reduce and control government spending, legislatively mandated changes in targeted agency/institution operations must occur in tandem with budget cuts. Just squeezing budgets won't work.

The good government notion of efficient government at the state level touted by Gil Carmichael and attempted by Barbour disappeared, usurped by antigovernment "starve-the-beast" believers. So, what about the "effective government" part of Gil's vision? I wrote about that.

REPUBLICANS OWN MALFUNCTION OF STATE GOVERNMENT

June 9, 2016

Republicans now dominate state government and own its performance.

Since 2004, the governor's office has been held by a Republican. Governors make most appointments to executive boards and agencies in Mississippi.

Lieutenant governors and speakers of the house make a limited number of appointments to Mississippi agency boards. Since 2002, a Republican has made every lieutenant governor appointment. Since 2012, a Republican has made every speaker of the house appointment.

Consequently, Republicans now control and own the performance of every state agency run by appointees.

For those state agencies run by elected officials, Republicans control all but the Office of Attorney General and the Public Service Commission.

The legislature provides the money and sets policy for the operation of state government. In January, Republicans gained a supermajority in the House of Representatives. That followed Republicans gaining a supermajority in the Senate four years earlier.

Consequently, Republicans now own the budget and overall performance of the legislature.

The stated goal of Republicans has been to rightsize government and make it perform more effectively and efficiently.

With Governor Phil Bryant, Lieutenant Governor Tate Reeves, and Speaker of the House Philip Gunn steering the ship and their minions running day-to-day operations, no doubt the consensus Republican plan to accomplish this goal is on track.

Houston, we have a problem.

There appears to be little trust or confidence between Republican legislators who control money and policy and Republican agency heads who run day-to-day operations. Nor is there any clear consensus about the role and function of state government. Bryant appears to be caught in the middle.

This disconnect among Republicans became highly visible during the recent legislative session and the resultant budget fiasco/retooling (pick one).

Republican Buck Clarke, chairman of the Senate Appropriations Committee, tried to explain the disconnect:

"There are many agencies providing valuable services to the citizens of this state, many funded at a level below what we would like. We also believe that each agency is sincere in their requests for funding as they and their advocates fight for their share of the pie. The truth of the matter is, though, that each agency and each advocate is not so concerned about funding levels at other agencies. However, it is our job in appropriations to be concerned with every agency and the mission with which they are charged."

Said another way, agency heads are not on board with legislative priorities.

Republican Commissioner of Insurance Mike Chaney, a former member of both the House and Senate, expressed frustrations shared by a number of agency heads.

"What we have had here is a failure to communicate," said Chaney. He told the *Clarion-Ledger* he tried to call Clarke twenty-seven times from March 22 through when lawmakers finished their work April 21 with no answer, "and it was the same with [House Appropriations Chairman] Herb Frierson."

What we have had this year is malfunctioning government fully owned by Republicans. Voters expected better.

Even as revenues picked up after the federal government infused billions of recovery dollars into state economies, agency heads continued to struggle with insufficient budgets in 2023. Several agency heads did remarkable jobs trimming staff and reordering duties while maintaining services. Others did not. Republicans failed to make government more effective, as Gil had hoped.

EXECUTIVE POWER

"A key to our ability to recover as quickly as we did came not only from preparation and from the character of the people affected but also from the uniform acceptance that someone had to be in charge," wrote Governor Haley Barbour in his acclaimed book "America's Great Storm: Leading through Hurricane Katrina." "With three coastal counties and eleven incorporated municipal governments, it would have been easy to have had competition for control by and among the local officials. Believe me, unlike in the business world where everyone recognizes that the CEO is

in charge, in the political world that is not a given. Despite the fact that I am a Republican and only the [state's] second GOP governor since 1876, and that many of the local officials were Democrats, it was universally accepted that the only 'someone' who could be in charge was the governor."

Haley Barbour may have been the last strong governor of Mississippi. Despite the limited constitutional powers of the office, the consummate pragmatist and dealmaker wielded what columnist Sid Salter described as "an outsized amount of power and influence." He harnessed the business community to his agenda and wielded power over the new Republican majority in the state Senate. However, executive power in state government declined considerably after Haley left office. I forecast those changes in 2011.

POLITICS TO RAMP UP AFTER ELECTION DAY

October 24, 2011

Mississippi has a weak governor system of governance. People have forgotten this under Haley Barbour's tenure because of his strong ties to the state Senate. The Mississippi constitution vests most power with the legislature.

Will Phil Bryant or Johnny DuPree wield power akin to Barbour's? Or, will tradition reassert itself and the inherent powers of the speaker of the house and lieutenant governor reemerge?

Mix in Billy McCoy's swan song as speaker and you get a recipe for consternation and confusion among lobbyists and political power players. As the public focuses on final campaigning for the November 8 general election, fervent behind-the-scenes campaigns are already being waged among current and potential state representatives who will choose the next speaker.

Remember, the speaker's race was decided four years ago by one flip-flop vote.

A key question here is which party will control the House. Will Democrats retain their majority or will Republicans take over? Who wins will determine whether there will be a grand reshuffling of committee chairmanships or not.

Multiple candidates from both parties want to be speaker. There appear to be no clear frontrunners. News reports list Democrat seekers as Bobby Moak, Cecil

Brown, Tyrone Ellis, and Preston Sullivan. Republican seekers include Jeff Smith, Philip Gunn, Sidney Bondurant, Mark Formby, Herb Frierson, and Mark Baker.

Now, stir in the uncertainty about reapportionment. Yep, the legislature still has to draw new voting districts to take into account population changes from the 2010 census. When they do, if they do, will the remap plan end up in federal court, will the federal court redraw districts again, and will there have to be interim legislative elections next year?

Depending on reapportionment and possible new election outcomes, there could be a do-over in the speaker's race. Wouldn't that make for interesting politics?

Waiting for the smoke to clear is all-but-certain lieutenant governor–elect Tate Reeves. He has only Reform Party candidate Tracella Lou O'Hara Hill as November opposition.

Reeves faces turnover in at least two top Senate leadership positions. President Pro Tem Billy Hewes gave up his post to run for lieutenant governor. Appropriations Committee chairman Doug Davis lost in his primary. Reeves has been traveling the state meeting with senators as he determines who will be on his leadership team. Will he move out or mix up committee chairmen or keep most in place?

What all this means is that politics won't wind down after Election Day. It's more likely to ramp up.

So, while the new governor will expect to lead the state and set the agenda, the new speaker and lieutenant governor will be staking out positions, testing their powers, and driving their own agendas. In this setting, personalities may override politics in the realignment of power.

Instead of a strong governor, Mississippi got all-powerful legislative leaders in Lieutenant Governor Tate Reeves and House Speaker Philip Gunn. As Republicans moved on to gain supermajorities in the Senate and House, rank-and-file legislators chose to, or got maneuvered to, adopt rules that ceded vast powers to their new leaders.

The most telling was an extraordinary rule change orchestrated in 2012 by incoming Gunn and Reeves. Joint Rule 20A required a legislator offering an amendment to increase appropriations for one agency to designate one or more other agencies to lose the same amount. Other restrictions made it almost impossible for rank-and-file members to amend appropriations bills. This rule proved to be particularly restrictive in years when the state had excess funds. Legislators could not tap those excess funds via amendments to increase spending. Changes could be made in conference, but the speaker and lieutenant governor controlled those decisions. Veteran capitol reporter Bobby Harrison said the rule gave the two leaders "unprecedented power."

It was no secret that Reeves and Gunn decided what legislation lived and which projects got funded (power Reeves grieved for when he assumed the weak governor's office). Ironically, Reeves and Gunn often exercised this power with little regard for, much less input from, rank-and-file members. I wrote about that in 2017.

CONCENTRATED POWER WAXING IN MISSISSIPPI LEGISLATURE

March 9, 2017

Concentrated power in the legislature waxes and wanes with the attitudes of rank-and-file members. At times, speakers of the house and lieutenant governors have wielded dictator-like power. At other times, members have risen up and made the bodies operate more democratically. Concentrated power is waxing once again as rank-and-file legislators cede power to their leaders.

The Mississippi constitution intends for the House and Senate to be deliberative bodies wherein the elected members discuss and debate the diverse views of their constituents as they formulate policy and law, not fiefdoms ruled by powerful lieutenant governors and speakers. Indeed, the constitution awards no strong powers to either office except that the lieutenant governor shall be the convening "president of the Senate." The vast power amassed in these offices is yielded by rank-and-file members through their rules and through tradition.

Lt. Gov. Tate Reeves displayed his dictator-like power last week when he announced that senators would not be allowed to consider House Bill 480. This is the bill to tax online sales. It was passed by the House and touted by Speaker Philip Gunn as a way to fund road and bridge improvements.

In his statement announcing that the Senate "will not consider a proposal to tax internet sales," Reeves argued that the bill may contravene a Supreme

Court ruling. That point was argued in the House (and in Alabama where the law is working), but its members, given the chance to decide for themselves, passed the bill. Using his power to enforce his personal position, Reeves denied senators the same opportunity.

Earlier in the session, Speaker Gunn played the same power game with regard to state lottery bills. As the Clarion-Ledger's Geoff Pender reported, "He's against it, and he doesn't even want the House to vote on it."

When Judiciary A Chairman Mark Baker had the audacity to ignore Gunn's feelings and pass out a lottery bill, Gunn "barged into the committee meeting and had a private meeting with Baker," Pender reported, adding it was not a cordial meeting.

The premature deaths of these revenue-enhancing bills come as the deterioration of state finances has reached an ominous stage.

"The state's economist and treasurer's office last week gave lawmakers a dour report on the state's economy," reported the *Clarion-Ledger* on February 21, "saying the state's growth and other economic indicators are lagging behind the nation, it has lost population, and state sales tax collections—its largest source of income—were at (minus) –0.5 percent for fiscal 2017 through January."

That was the same day Governor Phil Bryant announced his fifth "emergency midyear cut" and again dipped into the state's rainy day fund. A week earlier, State Treasurer Lynn Fitch revealed that Mississippi's bond debt jumped $1.3 billion to a total of $4.3 billion over ten years, a 43 percent increase (not including the state-guaranteed multibillion dollar PERS shortfall).

Outsiders looking at Mississippi and seeing revenue shortfalls, burgeoning debt, deteriorating roads, and power plays that abort possible solutions are unlikely to be attracted to our fair state.

It was also no secret that much of the legislation championed by Reeves and Gunn originated from outside the Mississippi legislature, often from outside the state. "Each year, state lawmakers across the US introduce thousands of bills dreamed up and written by corporations, industry groups and think tanks," reported Rob O'Dell and Nick Penzenstadler. "In all, these copycat bills amount to the nation's largest, unreported special-interest campaign, driving agendas in every statehouse and touching nearly every area of public policy." A major provider of "model bills" to state legislatures was the American Legislative Exchange Council (ALEC). Speaker Gunn served as ALEC's national chair in 2020.

"Mississippi leads nation in filing legislation that other people wrote," reported the *Clarion-Ledger*. "Between 2010 and 2018, Mississippi legislators introduced at least 744 model bills, *USA Today* found. That's 200 more model bills than the next highest state."

With so many bills coming from outsiders, not from Mississippi legislators, and the lieutenant governor and speaker deciding what passed, voters might wonder why they need to support 174 legislators. Alaska got by with sixty; Nebraska, forty-nine. Reducing the number of legislators could save millions of taxpayer dollars, shorten sessions, shrink government, and still yield voters the same results.

In 2019, I wrote a column entitled "Time to Change the Legislature One Way or Another," contending that whether voters deplored the way the Mississippi legislature currently operated or rejoiced in its good works, change was needed. Given Mississippi's needs, to maintain the status quo would verge on political insanity. Of course, nothing changed. Gil Carmichael's vision for a strong executive branch controlled by the governor did not just fade away, it flipped topsy-turvy—a hole in the whole that got bigger.

MISMANAGEMENT AND CORRUPTION

In 1977, columnist Wayne Weidie wrote about my opposition to corruption. "Crawford has won a bagful of newspaper awards, but even more important, Tallahatchie County politics hasn't been the same since the young editor moved to town. One need not agree with all of Crawford's editorials on local matters to know that in many cases he has just been presenting the public news which they have never been presented before."

My early newspaper career led me to understand and oppose mismanagement and corruption in government. That was one of the early attractions that drew me to Gil Carmichael's good government approach. In 1977, I won a Mississippi Press Association "best editorial in a weekly newspaper" award for my anticorruption opinion published in the Charleston *Sun-Sentinel.*

BOARD MOVE SURPRISING

November 11, 1976

What is government really all about?

The idea of government is to have an organization to do things for people that they can't do individually but that they recognize need to be done.

And, further, the idea of public officials is to have people of integrity and character to run the government. They must be people of high caliber because they must maintain public trust in government. For without faith in government there can be no effective government.

Unfortunately, history has shown that not all public officials are such beings of high caliber. Public servants from the president on down have proven to be susceptible to corruption, or at least too gullible to maintain public trust.

Consequently, laws have been passed to try and ensure public officials' conduct. Laws have been passed to let men know that if they get too imperfect, or too greedy, they will be called into account, and, in some cases, punished.

An example of such a law is the one in the Mississippi Code labeled Section 19-18-l. So important is this law, in fact, that similar language has been incorporated in the constitution of the State of Mississippi.

Simply put, this law forbids any public official from doing business with the board or agency of which he is a member.

Obviously, a member of a board could easily vote contracts for himself or such things and make a killing out of what is supposed to be service to the people.

So obscene is this threat of corruption to the public good that the law makes no exceptions . . . none whatsoever.

With this law so plain and forthright and so obviously for the public good, it is with great surprise that we learn our own county board of supervisors has voted, and indeed spread upon the public minutes of their actions their intention, to violate this law.

It does not matter that the board may think its action right and proper. It doesn't matter that no harm may have been done to the county or to the people of the county.

What matters is that the board would set a precedent by moving against the grain of one of the foundational laws of public trust in government.

When you make one exception, where do you draw the line on the next one?

And how can the board be so blatant as to move in the face of the law when the very matter now rests, as it should, in a court of law?

Is the board now above the law?

We urge every citizen to take all the personalities out of this controversy and to look at the law involved and see if they don't agree that the integrity of this law is essential to ensuring integrity in government.

And we hope every citizen will realize that those who will ignore the law in one case are hypocrites when they call for it to be exercised in another.

And that's telling it like it is.

As noted earlier, I supported Ray Mabus for governor in 1987 due in large part to his willingness to tackle corruption. Of course, mismanagement and corruption stayed with us. In 2014, *Forbes* magazine named Mississippi the most corrupt state in the nation. According to the article, the research studied more than twenty-five thousand convictions of public officials for violation of federal corruption laws between 1976 and 2008. When Republicans gained ultimate power over state government in 2012, not much changed.

After extensive bribery and corruption at the Mississippi Department of Corrections became public, Governor Phil Bryant in 2015 appointed his Task Force on Contracting and Procurement in the Mississippi Department of Corrections. I was one of five members. While a number of issues were presented to the task force, from start to finish we focused on steps needed to provide safeguards for taxpayer dollars. Lack of transparency, lack of oversight, and weak rules and systems were the key issues we had to address. Fortunately, we were able to tie a number of recommendations to legislation introduced by

Representative Jerry Turner. But several key recommendations were ignored by the legislature, including requiring the appropriate state agency (e.g., the Office of State Auditor or Ethics Commission) to conduct financial status reviews of state agency heads at least every four years and strengthening annual financial disclosure requirements for state agency heads.

The new contract review process Representative Turner got passed did go into effect. But problems remained. In 2017, the legislature abolished the Personal Service Contract Review Board and created a new Public Procurement Review Board under the Department of Finance and Administration. Representative Turner was still proposing bills to revamp the public contract review process in 2023.

In 2020, State Auditor Shad White announced his department had uncovered a multimillion dollar embezzlement and misappropriation of Temporary Assistance for Needy Families (TANF) federal funds controlled by the Mississippi Department of Human Services. Described as the worst in Mississippi history, the embezzlement centered on the Mississippi Community Education Center (MCEC). John Davis, the former Department of Human Services executive director, was arrested on charges of fraud and embezzlement. Davis had been appointed by Governor Phil Bryant and confirmed by Lieutenant Governor Tate Reeves's Senate. The MCEC's director, assistant director, and business manager were also arrested for embezzlement. Somehow, after Davis took over DHS in 2015, millions of federal TANF dollars found their way to the MCEC. White said TANF dollars were also used to fund a former wrestler's expensive rehab at a luxury clinic in Malibu and a volleyball facility at Davis's and Bryant's alma mater, the University of Southern Mississippi.

That same year, White reported on continued corruption in the prison system. In 2022, he told WLBT News that the auditor's office was uncovering government misuse of funds once a month. Much like Ray Mabus in the early 1980s, White made fighting corruption a high-profile task for his office, more so it seemed than other Republicans. I wrote about efforts to catch cheaters.

TO CATCH OR NOT CATCH CHEATERS?

November 13, 2022

During lunch at the North Jackson Rotary Club last Tuesday, State Auditor Shad White talked of his agency's efforts to catch people who steal taxpayers' money, a la Nancy New and the TANF scandal.

He also emphasized an initiative to stop people from cheating on Medicaid. White said he had talked the Republican-controlled legislature into giving his agents access to personal income tax returns. That allowed them to compare income reported on Medicaid applications to income reported on tax returns. He said they identified a number of cheaters who lied about income to Medicaid. "You don't want to lie on your tax returns," he said.

Hours later, newly reelected congressman Michael Guest told those gathered at his victory celebration what he expects a Republican takeover of the House of Representatives to accomplish.

"The first thing we're going to do is vote to defund the eighty-seven thousand IRS agents that were recently passed in the Democratic legislation," he said, as reported in the Clarion-Ledger. "We believe that those IRS agents, that the Democrats are seeking to unleash them on all the hardworking Americans."

Apparently, Guest and other Republicans don't want to aggressively catch people who cheat on their federal tax returns.

Hmmm.

Lying about income on Medicaid applications and lying about income on federal tax returns are both felonies. Strange to see one Republican official working assertively to catch cheaters while another is working assertively to avoid catching cheaters. Also strange to see a former district attorney take such a soft position on law and order.

A lot more can be unpacked from this.

One plays politics on the issue—Guest had a tough primary and, apparently, sees the need to appeal more to the Tea Party majority in the GOP base.

The other does not—White has gone after cheaters whatever their party affiliation and, apparently, sees no place for fraud and corruption in government.

A great many Republican voters in Mississippi see taxes as a form of government evil. So, politicians can cater to those feelings by limiting the capacity of the IRS to audit returns and catch cheaters.

A great many Republican voters in Mississippi see Medicaid as form of evil socialism. So, politicians can cater to those feelings by expanding the capacity to catch those who cheat Medicaid.

Still and all, cheaters are cheaters and White's desire to catch them is the honest approach.

The juxtaposition of these two conflicting approaches to cheaters on the same day as the nation's favorite cheater, former president Donald Trump, lost some of his clout was truly ironic. After a good number of Trump's chosen candidates outside of Mississippi lost or barely won, several Republicans proclaimed that these results would loosen Trump's leash on the party.

Maybe more Republicans at all levels of government can now stand up publicly for honesty.

"The integrity of the upright guides them, but the crookedness of the treacherous destroys them." —Proverbs 11:3

When Democrats controlled government in Mississippi, emerging Republicans condemned them for mismanagement and corruption. Overall, not much changed as Republicans gained control. Some state agency management did see notable improvements, though problems remained at others. As noted earlier, findings by State Auditor Shad White indicated corruption remained a problem through 2022 and into 2023.

TEA PARTY VS. GOOD GOVERNMENT

In "Federalist no. 62," constitution writer and future president James Madison explained that "good government" required two things: "first, fidelity to the object of government, which is happiness of the people; secondly, a knowledge of the means by which that object can best be attained." At the end of his second term, President Thomas Jefferson said, "The care of human life and happiness, and not their destruction, is the first and only legitimate object of good government."

While the Mississippi Republican Party toyed with Gil Carmichael's ideas early on and Haley Barbour's policies during his terms in office, it easily abandoned them when its base began to shift. Nothing signified the death of those ideas more than the party's embrace of the Tea Party's antigovernment, antitax mantras. Rather than Gil's and Haley's constructive good government conservatism, they preferred a form of destructive conservatism, something I wrote about in 2013.

ROCK-BRAIN POLITICS RUINING AMERICA

October 2, 2013

"If [reelection] means more to you than your country," he said, "when we need patriots to come out in a situation when we're in extremity, then you shouldn't even be in Congress."

That was former Wyoming senator Alan Simpson crying out for some "good 'ol common sense" in Washington, particularly from his former Republican colleagues.

"Common sense . . . seems to escape members of our party," he said.

Don't misunderstand. Simpson is as much against Obamacare—the root of the current constipation in Washington these days—as the next Republican.

"It can't work, because all you have to do is use common sense," he said, pointing to the costs to sustain it.

But, he's not willing to mulishly decimate America over that one issue. The unwillingness of leaders to find commonsense compromises on the budget and the debt ceiling galls Simpson. As does their willingness to put the economic well-being of citizens at risk as they posture for reelection.

"If you want to be in politics, you learn to compromise," he said. "Show me a guy who won't compromise and I'll show you a guy with rocks for brains."

Common sense, not rock-brain posturing, helped the United States to its extraordinary position as the world's shining example of functional democracy. Alexis de Tocqueville wrote Democracy in America, volume 1, in 1835, hailing Americans' "strength and common sense." President Dwight Eisenhower in 1956 linked American common sense and politics, saying, "I do not believe that any political campaign justifies the declaration of a moratorium on ordinary common sense."

Simpson was a friend and colleague of the late Sonny Montgomery. He, Sonny, and the late senator John Stennis exemplified patriotic leaders willing to use common sense and put America first, ahead of politics and self-interest.

Today, allies wonder if our democratic republic will ever function properly again. Enemies see us as vulnerable and growing weaker. An extended government shutdown plus a government default over the debt ceiling would cause more harm to America than anything dreamed of by Iran, al-Qaeda, or Karl Marx.

And, it would be self-inflicted ruin.

In 1814, former president John Adams warned, "There never was a democracy yet that did not commit suicide."

Speaking of rock-brain Republicans, did you see the story published in CQ Roll Call about the Tea Party darling state senator considering a primary challenge to Senator Thad Cochran? When asked about such a challenge, little-known Chris McDaniel of Ellisville said, "We are keeping all of our options open because we want to do the right thing for the conservative movement."

The right thing "for the conservative movement," he said, not "for America" or even "for Mississippi."

Shall we now pledge allegiance to the conservative movement?

Pray for less nonsense and more commonsense patriotism.

After the national Tea Party gained notoriety in 2009, Mississippi members began planning to take down Republican congressmen and senators they saw as not conservative enough. They had twisted conservative ideology into a shameful political paradigm where it was better to lose than get a partial win through compromise; where ideologues who got nothing done got accolades, while leaders trying to follow Ronald Reagan's example of horse trading to move a conservative agenda ahead got primaried; and where casting blame counted for more than winning concessions. This came to fruition in Mississippi when Tea Party champion State Senator Chris McDaniel decided to take on US Senator Thad Cochran, another Republican good government champion and constructive conservative. I wrote about this in 2013.

TEA PARTY PREFERS INFLEXIBLE DISSIDENTS

October 23, 2013

Senator Roger Wicker must be anxiously watching the Tea Party blitz against fellow Senator Thad Cochran. The two senators have much in common.

For example, until they were banned by House Republicans, Wicker's record for delivering earmarks was second only to Cochran's. The Tea Party claims earmarks were a major factor in escalating deficits. They weren't, but the claim is pervasive.

Wicker has been a recent champion of bipartisan deal-making. In July he called for concessions by both parties to avoid the "nuclear option" rules change Sen. Majority Leader Harry Reid had proposed to thwart Republican filibusters. Additionally, as a member of the Senate Budget Committee and, thus, a participant on the House-Senate conference committee charged with recommending a compromise budget by mid-December, Wicker told the Clarion-Ledger:

"The public expects us to show that we are problem solvers, and they want a result. And, I hope that is something we can deliver on in a bipartisan fashion."

The Tea Party, however, considers any bipartisan deals as "sabotage by weak Republicans." When Cochran voted for the bipartisan deal to reopen government, the Tea Party called Cochran "pathetic" and said he "continually votes against the wishes of his constituents." Wicker also voted to reopen government.

It's clear that the Tea Party prefers inflexible dissidents of the Ted Cruz breed rather than negotiator statesmen of the Cochran and Wicker style.

Conservative writer George Will recently described how James Madison, father of the US constitution, intended out government to work:

"Madison created a constitutional regime that by its structure created competing power centers and deprived any of them of the power to impose its will on the others." This system of politics, said Will, forces politicians "to bargain and collaborate."

"Recently Washington has been tumultuous because politics, as the Framers understood it, has disintegrated," said Will.

How ironic that the Tea Party says it champions the constitution while at the same time promoting politicians who would destroy its intended operation.

It appears that the Tea Party prefers politicians who rant, shut down the government, and hold the economy hostage while those who created our constitution preferred politicians who negotiate, restrain government, and keep the economy on a path to growth. Indeed, the practical solution to our deficit and debt crises is to restrain the growth in government spending (including Medicare and Social Security) while increasing the growth of our economy (which would generate more tax revenue). Brinksmanship and shutdowns hinder growth; negotiated long-term restraint would spur it.

Heretofore, Wicker and Cochran—as did their predecessors Trent Lott, John Stennis, and Jim Eastland—have followed the path our Founders intended.

Which path do Mississippi voters now prefer?

The hard-fought primary and the vitriolic runoff won by Cochran in 2014 caused a split in the party. That split was bolstered by the rise of something I call "truth management."

TRUTH MANAGEMENT

An alpha and omega difference exists between tellers and teachers. Tellers tell for their benefit. Teachers teach for our benefit. Tellers would do our thinking, planning, meditating, praying, and, yes, deciding for us. The rise of the tellers on cable TV, talk radio, internet blogs and blasts, and values and lifestyle books fills the gap for us. Instant how-to-think, what-matters, what-to-pray-for, and what-to-do input! Teachers help us to study, to seek, to discover, to try, to experience, and, most importantly, to decide for ourselves.

With the images it provokes, the song "Coat of Many Colors" by Dolly Parton is a metaphor for the roughhewn fabric of twentieth-century America as it was woven through hardship, hard work, and hardy devotion. This uniquely American fabric of many colors, races, and creeds was a tie that bound us together; *e pluribus unum*, our founding fathers named it. But there are slashes, holes, and pricks that tear away at this fabric, particularly our modern phenomenon of 24/7 political and media personalities who prosper by inciting others to slash, punch, and prick our national fabric. Can it hold together, this fabric of ours? Can it hold us together? Or, should we be asking, can we hold it together?

The US Supreme Court's controversial 5 to 4 ruling in 2010 allowing unregulated corporate electioneering in the *Citizens United* case and the derivative decision in the US Court of Appeals, DC Circuit, prohibiting limits for contributions to super PACS allowed big money not just to dominate elections but to finance giant propaganda machines. That, coupled with the rise of the Tea Party, presaged the powerful influence national antitax, antigovernment political interest groups would wield on Mississippi politics. In 2014, forty-two super-wealthy individuals gave $200 million to super PACs to "shape" the midterm elections, according to *USA Today*. That was nearly one-third of the $615 million accumulated by all super PACs for the 2014 elections. Most of this money sought to shape contests between Republicans and Democrats. But some went to shape races between incumbent Republicans and Republican challengers. About $9 million was used to shape the bitter battle between challenger Chris McDaniel and incumbent senator Thad Cochran.

How the super wealthy used super PACs to shape elections to suit their interests became big business. There are the media firms that produce the super PACs' TV spots. There are talented direct mail firms they can hire to use demographic information, voting history, and algorithms to tailor messages directly to individuals and groups. There are robocall firms that send tailored messages to home phones. There are social media firms with talented staffs and sophisticated data and polling systems who focus every day on crafting messages that go out through bloggers, political subgroups, Twitter, Facebook, and, most recently, cell phone texts. Super PACs also hire influence leaders who persuade networks of talking heads and political junkies to get their messages out. Artificial intelligence will raise this shadowy practice to new heights.

I wrote about the rising threat from social media.

CAN CIVIC EDUCATION SAVE DEMOCRACY FROM SOCIAL MEDIA?

January 6, 2020

As two of the three branches of government become more and more politicized, the posture of the third will play a crucial role in how our federal government works.

The two politicized branches, of course, are the executive and legislative. The third, supposed to always rise above politics, is the judicial branch.

Last week, US Supreme Court Chief Justice John Roberts spoke on behalf of the judicial branch.

"We have come to take democracy for granted," he wrote in his year-end report, "and civic education has fallen by the wayside.

"In our age, when social media can instantly spread rumor and false information on a grand scale, the public's need to understand our government, and the protections it provides, is ever more vital."

Many among the highly politicized deemed Roberts's comments a swipe at President Donald Trump and other highly visible politicians, and at blatantly biased media.

Maybe, but what Roberts appeared to truly mean is, we as a nation are not preparing citizens with the proper knowledge and orientation to decipher truth from political propaganda.

"Civic education, like all education, is a continuing enterprise and conversation," he wrote. "Each generation has an obligation to pass on to the next, not only a fully functioning government responsive to the needs of the people, but the tools to understand and improve it."

In plain terms, he means that social media is not an honest source for civic education.

The intended source is public education—schools, colleges, and universities. Indeed, that is why free public education was promoted by our founding fathers.

"Educate and inform the whole mass of the people," wrote Thomas Jefferson. "Enable them to see that it is their interest to preserve peace and order, and they will preserve them. And it requires no very high degree of education to convince them of this. They are the only sure reliance for the preservation of our liberty."

(Personal note: the late Mary Brooks of Jackson taught me this in high school. As one who believed passionately in civic education and responsibility, she would be aghast at today's civic illiteracy.)

Johns Hopkins University president Ronald J. Daniels believes universities hold the key to civic education in modern times.

"Alarming numbers of young people struggle to distinguish reliable information from misinformation online," he wrote last week, "and the public's faith in core democratic institutions—and fellow citizens—is eroding more by the day."

Calling for higher education to provide a "truly robust civic education," he said such must include "a grasp of the history and theory of democracy to bring a nuanced understanding of the past to public life, and critical reasoning skills that help to distinguish true information from false." He also included "a commitment to values such as tolerance and equality that provide standards against which to hold policymakers and policies to account, and a disposition directed toward cooperation and action."

Roberts and Daniels, like Jefferson, propound a clarion call to reason in the face of growing unreason. Amid today's politicized cacophony, who will hear their call, much less heed it?

"For the time will come when people will not put up with sound doctrine. Instead, to suit their own desires, they will gather around them a great number of teachers to say what their itching ears want to hear. They will turn their ears away from the truth and turn aside to myths." —2 Timothy 4:3–4

In 2016, I wrote about the Charles Koch Foundation spending millions to shape thinking on college campuses, including Mississippi State University. Koch money also funded nonprofit groups advocating the Koch agenda, including conservative state-based think tanks affiliated with the national State Policy Network such as the Mississippi Center for Public Policy. The Koch network continued funding the State Policy Network and its affiliated American Legislative Exchange Council on which Mississippi Speaker of the House Philip Gunn served as a board member. School choice advocate Empower Mississippi was linked to this network. The Mississippi chapter of Americans for Prosperity, a Koch-founded organization, rose to dominate thinking on many legislative issues. The chapter strongly touted Lieutenant Governor Tate Reeves when he promoted its agenda.

What these powerful shapers do has a name—truth management. I wrote about truth management several times.

TRUTH MANAGERS SKEW REALITY

January 16, 2016

Since the earliest days of civilization, "truth management" has been practiced by governments and religions to further their own interests. Decades ago, the Soviet Union's disinformation and revisionist history activities stood out. Today, truth management pervades international communications, with Putin's Russia, Iran, North Korea, and ISIL among the standouts.

The practice of truth management has proliferated to organizations throughout the United States, too, and now pervades presidential politics.

Envision a persuasion scheme that integrates widespread publicity, rampant disinformation, and tailored "truths." That's truth management.

Our Defense Department has long practiced "perception management" and "truth projection" to influence beliefs—usually foreign but not always.

More recently, well-funded national policy institutes and research centers have emerged that propagate research and findings supportive of preconceived notions—they tailor "truth" to fit stipulated concepts. These perverted truths are shared with bloggers, talking heads, publicity organizations, and lobbyists who adeptly use them to manipulate the public, politicians, and policymakers into believing and proclaiming such as actual truths.

Consider this excerpt from a study of the tobacco industry published by the Department of Social and Behavioral Sciences, School of Nursing, University of California:

"This study adds to the growing literature that draws upon previously secret tobacco industry documents to understand the inner workings of the industry. Previous research has, among other things, revealed how the industry has deceived the public and policymakers about the harms of tobacco, manipulated science, used third parties to promote its agenda, targeted vulnerable populations, and interfered with regulatory and public policy processes. These behaviors are not unique to the tobacco industry; research on internal asbestos and chemical industry documents has uncovered similar actions."

The tobacco companies managed truth by getting institutes and research centers, which they funded directly and indirectly, to publish studies showing tobacco usage to be not very harmful. They then used these deceitful studies and powerful publicity to manipulate users and politicians into believing that smoking was safe.

Today's institutes and research centers funded by billionaires to further their agendas are expanding this approach. Social media, the internet, and talk radio thrive on their work product.

Senators, congressmen, and their staffs are too busy to do much research. So, they rely on information from lobbyists who get their information from these biased sources.

Policy institutes and research centers actuated by preconceived notions have begun cropping up to shape "truth" at the state level, too. Legislators have even less time and resources than congressmen to research complex issues.

Folks, it's one thing to use facts that support arguments and overlook facts that don't. It's quite another to deliberately create and disseminate false truths that skew reality. And that's what insidious truth managers do.

So, whether it's Donald Trump or Hillary Clinton, the NRA or the AARP, big business or big government, or a state policy institute, realize that their propensity to engage in truth management is for their benefit, not yours.

Syndicated columnist Mona Charen called truth managers "conflict entrepreneurs," in 2022. "You know them," she wrote. "They are the arsonists who incessantly inflame every disagreement in order to boost their own 'brands.' They rile us up and deceive us about the danger of 'the other side.'"

"Democracy demands an informed electorate," stated Ilya Somin in a policy analysis published by the Cato Institute in 2004. "Voters who lack sufficient knowledge may be manipulated" by opinion leaders who "have strong incentives to exaggerate the importance of political problems." Knowing what some well-paid commentator touts as the latest cause on Fox News, MSNBC, or talk radio is not the same as being informed. Don't count on politicians' "talking points" or your favorite blogs, tweets, or websites, either. Ignorance of the truth allows people to be led by the nose like cows to slaughter. Without real knowledge, people have no context to weigh the benefits of "causes" or strong arguments against. They become ready prey to those seeking power. "If we are to guard against ignorance and remain free, as Jefferson cautioned, it is the responsibility of every American to be informed," as Ronald Reagan said during National Library Week in 1981.

From my perspective, years of truth management efforts by the likes of the Club for Growth, Americans for Tax Reform, and Tea Party Express wreaked havoc in the Republican Party. They challenged and undermined GOP incumbents and party leaders who were "soft" on their issues. Often their narrow-mindedness showed a preference for martyrs over winners and inaction over incremental gains favored by the likes of Haley Barbour. They used conspiracy theories and truth management techniques through conservative and social media to build huge constituencies of mistrusting "aginners." Their destructive approach drove feelings about government beyond discontent to hostility. It is one thing to disagree. It is quite another to dislike or hate. Frustration is rational; hostility is irrational. This played well in already mistrustful Mississippi.

Ultimate havoc came with the election of Donald Trump as president in 2016. A gifted truth manager, Trump seized control of the angry Republican base with his "Make America Great Again" agenda. He amped up attacks on GOP incumbents and party leaders who failed to ally with him. He magnified the impact of conspiracy theories and truth management techniques through his tweets and at MAGA rallies.

I wrote about the dangers of conspiracism in 2021.

CONSPIRACISM UNDERMINES CIVIL SOCIETY

June 13, 2021

Real conservatives know who Peggy Noonan is. Read her latest column, "What Drives Conspiracism," where she laments that irrational conspiracies "fueled and powered" by the internet are "helping break up America."

Rational people know that civil society cannot work when leadership embraces conspiracism. Rather, civil society requires civil leadership.

Flashback: Ronald Reagan defined civil society as order with virtue. Reagan was also the epitome of civil leadership—strong but conciliatory, demanding but willing to compromise, conservative but willing to work across party lines.

Reagan said, "Our first president, George Washington, Father of our Country, shaper of the constitution and truly a wise man, believed that religion, morality, and brotherhood were the essential pillars of society."

Reagan also affirmed the prayer embodied in America the Beautiful—"America! America! God shed his grace on thee, and crown thy good with brotherhood from sea to shining sea!"

For him, brotherhood transcended politics, as demonstrated by his legendary relationship with Tip O'Neill, the Democratic Speaker of the House. O'Neill's son Thomas described their relationship, their commitment to "find common ground," this way:

"What both men deplored more than the other's political philosophy was stalemate, and a country that was so polarized by ideology and party politics that it could not move forward" (sound familiar?).

"While neither man embraced the other's world view, each respected the other's right to hold it. Each respected the other as a man."

The late congressman G. V. "Sonny" Montgomery also bought into the notion that brotherhood should transcend politics. His relationship with Republican president George H. W. Bush is also legendary.

"When it came to matters affecting our national security and matters of war and peace, we stood as one," Bush wrote in the foreword to Sonny's memoir The Veteran's Champion.

The late Sen. John C. Stennis may be the best twentieth-century example of civil leadership. Stennis was respected for his character, steadfast faith in God, and love for people.

Reagan said of Stennis, "The humble man who came to Washington from a small town in Mississippi has made an impression on American government that is difficult to measure and hard to fully describe. He has demonstrated for all of us that one man, committed to God and country, willing to work hard and sacrifice personal gain and comfort, can make a difference."

"He considered it a point of pride, not weakness, to be able to work across the aisle with presidents of the other party," said William "Brother" Rogers, former associate director of the John C. Stennis Center for Public Service.

"When we face difficult times, difficult issues," Reagan said, "we Americans can unite for the common good." Montgomery and Stennis would agree.

Flash forward: But today's snarly politics would not.

As civil leadership wanes in our national leaders, what does that foretell for state and local leadership? For our national fabric and civil society?

Conspiracism that brews hateful rhetoric and anarchy and breaks up America.

And, as Noonan warns, "conspiracism isn't going away. It will only grow and become damaging in ways we aren't quite imagining."

Unless true patriots stand up for brotherhood and civil leadership.

"Let your conversation be always full of grace, seasoned with salt, so that you may know how to answer everyone." —Colossians 4:6

Trump's attacks let him take control of the Republican Party and its agenda. His approach also led many Republican politicians down a perverse path where they publicly praised Trump to retain voter support while privately disparaging him.

As Trumpism and shaped messaging poured into Mississippi, more and more mainstream Mississippi politicians—Thad Cochran's successor, Senator Cindy Hyde-Smith; the three Republican congressmen; and most state officials—gravitated to the partisan, antigovernment approach commandeered by Trump. Senator Roger Wicker, an early Carmichael supporter, also tacked in that direction but showed some independence—for instance, he voted against Trump's national emergency declaration to build a border wall and for President Joe Biden's Bipartisan Infrastructure Law.

Viewing the direction of the Republican Party in 2020, Stuart Stevens, the media whiz who helped elect Thad Cochran to the Senate, wrote an opinion piece titled "Wake Up, Republicans. Your Party Stands for All the Wrong Things Now." Dismayed former ardent Republicans said Trump had taken over the party and turned it into a cult.

The growth of the truth management industry in parallel with social media and the rise of Donald Trump resulted in effective messaging that decimated trust, promoted factionalism, subverted penchants for good government conservatism, and punched new holes in the whole in Mississippi. What a twisted situation, especially for a largely Christian state where pastors preach "love your neighbor and your enemy" and Republicans preach Christian heritage.

A COMPETITIVE TWO-PARTY SYSTEM

Some weeks after 1972 rolled around, the GOP began searching for quality candidates to run for congressional seats being vacated by Representatives William Colmer, Tom Abernethy, and Charles Griffin. Maurice Dantin had been reapportioned out of Colmer's Fifth District, or he might have been approached by the Republicans since he was a Colmer favorite. But that lot fell to Colmer's administrative assistant, Trent Lott. He, Thad Cochran, and Carl Butler of Columbus were convinced by GOP leaders that the party's organization and money-raising capabilities were strong enough to go with Nixon's coattails to bring wins in November. They also were offered clear paths into the November elections, avoiding hard-fought Democratic primaries.

In the 1970s, Gil Carmichael's popular appeal and successes by Thad Cochran and Trent Lott spurred Republican Party growth. Gil's goal to build a competitive two-party system became a reality in the 1980s. Republicans started winning state and local elections, though without the Black voters Gil and Charles sought.

In 1988, Trent Lott won the seat vacated by longtime Senator John Stennis. In 1991, Kirk Fordice became the first Republican governor since Reconstruction, and Republican Eddie Briggs was elected lieutenant governor. In 1995, Fordice was reelected, but Democrats regained the lieutenant governor post. In 1999, Democrats took back nearly all of the eight statewide offices, but Republican Phil Bryant was elected as state auditor. In 2003, Republicans won several posts: Haley Barbour as governor, Amy Tuck as lieutenant governor (after her party switch), Bryant as state auditor, and Tate Reeves as state treasurer. In 2005, Secretary of Agriculture and Commerce Lester Spell switched parties.

Things changed in 2007, when Republicans won all but one of the statewide positions. Barbour was reelected governor, Bryant won as lieutenant governor, Delbert Hosemann won as secretary of state, Stacey Pickering won as state auditor, Mike Chaney won as insurance commissioner, Reeves won again as state treasurer, and Spell won again as secretary of agriculture and commerce. Republicans continued to hold those offices until they finally won the attorney general position in 2019 and took control of all statewide positions in 2020.

Along the way, Republicans began to win more and more seats in the legislature, regional commissions, and city and county government. The party took permanent control of the Senate in 2011 and the House in 2012. Both gained supermajorities just a few years later.

Since then, Republicans have come to dominate politics just as the Democrats did years ago and, disappointingly, in much the same manner. I wrote about that.

MISSISSIPPI GOP BECOMES WHAT EARLY LEADERS FOUGHT

November 22, 2020

Impressions from then and now . . .

Forty-three years ago when I first began writing a weekly political column, several focused on the new Republicanism emerging in Mississippi as portrayed by party leaders. They described a surging party intent on building a strong two-party system in Mississippi. A strong two-party system was the goal of longtime party builder Clarke Reed. "From now on the best man will win no matter which party he belongs to," he said.

He had just turned the party chairmanship over to "young, handsome Laurel attorney Charles Pickering," the lone Republican in the Mississippi state Senate. Pickering was seen as "a young, aggressive force for good government in Mississippi."

"No tunnel-vision reactionary," I wrote, "Pickering speaks of Republicanism that retains its commitment to fiscal responsibility but that addresses itself to the needs for charity and opportunity for the poor."

"Two Thursdays ago, State Republican Chairman Charles Pickering and GOP leader Gil Carmichael spoke to an NAACP gathering in Jackson," I wrote later. "Their visit typifies the GOP commitment to include Blacks in the Mississippi party."

At that time, I was the young editor of a weekly paper in Tallahatchie County, but also the GOP county chairman. I was among many young Mississippians tired of the stagnant, prejudiced, one-party domination of Big Jim Eastland's Democratic Party.

Zip ahead forty-three years and what do we find?

One-party domination sticks out the most. The concept of a strong two-party system has faded from Republican rhetoric. Reed's "best man wins" concept is far less important than party label, as it was back then. Indeed, the dominant GOP base of voters today much resembles that of Big Jim's Democratic Party.

Back then, too, Speaker Buddie Newman, a staunch Eastland ally, wielded autocratic control over the Mississippi House of Representatives. Today, Speaker Philip Gunn does much the same. He controls major legislation with an iron fist and lack of transparency similar to Newman's.

The concepts of "good government" with "fiscal responsibility" that addressed "the needs for charity and opportunity for the poor" seem gone with the wind. That focus has given way to the old ways of "political government" and "fiscal favors," with token crumbs for those in need. Nothing, perhaps, depicts this better than Governor Tate Reeves's call last week for more tax cuts in the face of huge needs in health care and schools in the face of the COVID-19 pandemic, growing crises in our prisons and hospitals, continued critical needs for road and bridge repairs, and so on.

The fervor for a strong-two party system among early Republicans forty-three years ago was tangible. One of those early Republicans from east Mississippi contended that one-party domination of Mississippi government was similar to Communist Party domination in the Soviet Union.

Those leaders, today, would chime in with cartoonist Walt Kelly's swamp character Pogo, who quipped in 1970, "We have met the enemy and he is us."

"Do not boast about tomorrow, for you do not know what a day may bring." —Proverbs 27:1

Republicans closed a dire hole, then reopened it wider and deeper. That well characterized the end of what began as a hopeful journey to build a party capable of and eager to close holes in the whole.

SUMMARY

Gil Carmichael and Haley Barbour pursued a good government approach to governing aimed at improving the lives of all Mississippians. Following Haley's terms as governor, the party turned to a strange melding of old Democratic Party methods and modern Tea Party populism.

Upon Gil's death in 2016, the *Northeast Mississippi Daily Journal* wrote: "Political leaders like Carmichael, grounded in the private sector and visionary about governance, walk among us seldom. Carmichael caused many Mississippians to rethink what kind of state we seek for all citizens."

Just not enough such thinkers, particularly within his own party.

Gil failed to get it done, and others after him. But his moral and constructive good government ideas remain as a guide to pry Mississippi off the bottom in the future:

- Write a new, moral constitution to reorganize and rightsize government and to strengthen executive power;
- Run rightsized government like a business to eliminate waste, mismanagement, and corruption. Utilize savings from those efficiencies to make necessary programs effective and to uplift Mississippi's disadvantaged through improved schools and better jobs;
- Build a competitive two-party system to produce better government policy; and
- Diversify the Republican Party to pull people together.

Chapter Two

SPLOTCHY PATTERNS OF SHADOW AND LIGHT

THE LEFT OUT AND LEFT BEHIND

A course I took at the American University School of International Service was taught by a crusty old fellow named Sam Sharpe. He was a refugee from eastern Europe and an expert consultant on Soviet affairs to the State Department. (He was also a grand master bridge player.) I wrote a paper analyzing India's famous international policy of nonaggression under Nehru as compared to its brutal takeover of Portuguese Goa. My conclusion was that India's policy was hypocritical and that India should be judged by its deeds, not its words. I'll never forget when Mr. Sharpe gave me back my paper with an A+, telling me this was a good lesson to remember in regard to any government.

As Republicans completed eleven years of control over state government, how did things stand in Mississippi in 2023; was the state better or worse for Republicans' fifty-year climb into power? That depended upon your source of information—politicians or data.

In 2022, new Mississippi Republican Party Chairman Frank Bourdeaux published an opinion column in newspapers across the state entitled "Nation Should Follow Mississippi's Conservative Example." In it, he extolled Governor Tate Reeves and Republican legislative leaders for having "balanced the budget, grown the economy, and reduced unemployment." He said Republican leadership was "producing real results for their citizens."

A different source of information, national rankings based on data analysis, showed Mississippi making little progress and still stuck on the bottom.

TOPIC	RANK	SOURCE
ECONOMIC		
Average wages	50	US Bureau of Labor Statistics
Workforce participation rate	50	Federal Reserve Bank of St. Louis report
Per capita income	50	US Census American Community Survey
Median family income	50	US Census American Community Survey
Children in poverty	50	US Census American Community Survey
Economy	49	*US News & World Report* Best States report
Poverty	49	*US News & World Report* Best States report
Economic opportunity	49	*US News & World Report* Best States report
Workforce educational attainment	48	US Census American Community Survey
Business environment	48	*US News & World Report* Best States report
Jobs in high-tech industry	47	WalletHub.com report
Economic growth	44	*US News & World Report* Best States report
EDUCATION		
Academic investment	50	US Census American Community Survey
Academic performance	49	Intelligent.com report
Educational attainment	49	WalletHub.com report
Quality of education	49	WalletHub.com report
STEM education	49	Academicful.com report
College readiness	49	*US News & World Report* Best States report
Average ACT scores	48	Intelligent.com report
Pre-K through 12	44	*US News & World Report* Best States report
HEALTH CARE		
Health care outcomes	50	WalletHub.com report
Life expectancy	50	CDC National Center for Health Statistics
Infant mortality	50	CDC National Center for Health Statistics
Maternal mortality	50	Centers for Disease Control & Prevention
Teen pregnancy	50	CDC National Center for Health Statistics

TOPIC	RANK	SOURCE
Births to unwed mothers	50	CDC National Center for Health Statistics
Low birthweight babies	50	CDC National Center for Health Statistics
Preterm births	50	CDC National Center for Health Statistics
Child health	50	Kids Count Data Book report
Elderly health care	50	America's Health Rankings report
All causes of death	50	National Institutes of Health
Child obesity	50	Centers for Disease Control & Prevention
Births to teens	49	CDC National Center for Health Statistics
Deaths from heart disease	49	CDC National Center for Health Statistics
Nursing home quality	49	*US News & World Report* Best States report
Preventable hospitalizations	48	America's Health Rankings report
Access to mental health care	47	Mental Health America report
Adult obesity	47	Centers for Disease Control & Prevention
Public health	46	*US News & World Report* Best States report
Uninsured adults	46	US Census SAHIE Program
Health care affordability	46	*US News & World Report* Best States report
Health care access	45	*US News & World Report* Best States report
OTHER		
Quality of life	50	WalletHub.com report
Incarcerations per capita	50	Bureau of Justice Statistics
Public school safety	50	WalletHub.com report
Road safety	50	WalletHub.com report
Food insecurity	50	America's Health Rankings report
Population growth	49	US Census American Community Survey
Homicide rate	49	National Institutes of Health
Child well-being	48	Kids Count Data Book report
Workplace safety	48	WalletHub.com data
Internet access	48	*US News & World Report* Best States report
Infrastructure	47	*US News & World Report* Best States report
Healthy food environment	46	USDA Food Environment Atlas report
Most current rankings as of October 15, 2023		

These bottom rankings pointed to numerous holes in another type of "whole." The Mississippi constitution says that our state government exists "solely for the good of the whole." It gives state government the constitutional power and the constitutional purpose to provide services Mississippians need. "The whole," of course, means all the people, not some of the people or just the people in power. Balancing the needs of the poor and the rich, the old and the young, the coast and the hills, and so on, for the benefit of the whole is the great challenge of state government. It is the raison d'être for good government leadership.

The last governor to address this issue was Haley Barbour. In his inaugural address to the legislature in 2004 he said, "If any area, or any group of people is left out, it holds back the rest of the state." Our many bottom rankings indicate that many in Mississippi have been left out.

Generally, we have considered as left out those living in poverty. The United Way's ALICE project (Asset Limited, Income Constrained, and Employed) reported that, in Mississippi, many more have been left behind. The ALICE National Overview estimated that 52 percent of Mississippi households were left out or left behind—20 percent living below the poverty line plus another 32 percent too poor to afford the basics of housing, child care, food, transportation, health care, and technology due to low wages (2021 numbers). Mississippi United Way organizations joined the national ALICE network to give underpaid, hardworking Mississippians a voice.

We have also usually considered those without a high school degree as left out. But in today's economy, those with just a high school diploma or general education diploma (GED) often get left behind, only able to qualify for low-skill, low-wage jobs. The 2021 census American Community Survey (ACS) showed 44 percent of Mississippi's adult population left out or left behind—14 percent without a high school degree plus another 30 percent with only a high school degree or GED. A CNBC analysis found Mississippi's workforce to be the second-least educated in the nation, ranking just above West Virginia.

We have tended to think of poor Delta counties as those most left out. But data shows many more counties left out and left behind, particularly rural counties. "Smaller, rural communities are still struggling to maintain and grow," explained David Rumbarger, president and CEO of the Community Development Foundation in Lee County. The bipartisan Economic Innovation Group studied trends in rural counties across America. It reported seventy-three of Mississippi's eighty-two counties in decline based on trends for seven criteria: (1) the percentage of the adult population with no high school diploma; (2) the housing vacancy rate; (3) the percentage of working-age adults who are not working; (4) the poverty rate; (5) the ratio of county income over state income; (6) the change in number of jobs; and (7) the change in number of businesses. Sixty-one of sixty-four counties served by the Delta Regional Authority and the Appalachian Regional Commission were rated economically distressed. Poverty rates in forty-three of Mississippi's eighty-two counties persisted at 20 percent or more for over thirty years (1990 to 2020). Not surprisingly, census data showed that sixty-four of Mississippi's eighty-two counties lost population from 2010 to 2020. Physician shortages coupled with nursing shortages were among the other issues causing rural distress.

With so many left out and left behind, it was no wonder Mississippi ranked at or near the bottom in so many measures.

MISSISSIPPI SHADOWS

From my lifelong perspective, we Mississippians, like catfish, tend to venerate shade. But ours may be blessed shade from the sweltering sun or impious shade from glaring truth. So, we meander down literal and figurative shady lanes daubed with splotchy patterns of shadow and light. We dawdle in the shade to avoid the patches of hot sunlight and linger in the shadows to dodge truth's harsh radiance.

So, what is it about us in Mississippi that we tolerate such bottom dwelling as blithely as river catfish? That we perpetuate the holes of inefficient, ineffective, mismanaged, often corrupt government to keep us there? That we adhere to shaded truths and reject whole notions of good government that could lift us up? Have we simply become indifferent to the stark consequences revealed by our bottom rankings?

Why we do what we do seems to lie in the commingling of three areas I label Faulkner's curse, the double whammy, and insanity.

FAULKNER'S CURSE

"Don't you see?" said Faulkner's character Isaac McCaslin in "The Bear." "This whole land, the whole South, is cursed, and all of us who derive from it, whom it ever suckled, white and black both, lie under the curse."

My older cousin Dudley Crawford, now a retired Presbyterian minister, recalled what our culture taught and expected when we were growing up back in the 1950s. "Daddy's mother was the one called to sit with the ill and dying," Dudley wrote. "At the crack of dawn every morning she and her near sister, a Black helper named Josephine Readirs, would bake tea rings and other goods to deliver to shut-ins around town." He remembers that Mamaw and Josephine were "thick as thieves" and how Josephine was "family enough" to stay with Mamaw for decades until her death in the local nursing home. "As a little child, I had difficulty understanding the difference between Black and white and just where Josephine stood. I remember asking her to sit with us at the children's table during one of Mamaw's Thanksgiving dinners. She said she couldn't, as did Mama and Mamaw. I simply took my plate and joined her on the back porch bench for a real American Thanksgiving." Older, Dudley would remember: "It was one of those preexisting congenital conditions of southern living and/or dying. Thanks to the Klan, the White Citizens' Council, Hederman Press, and the Mississippi Sovereignty Commission, everyone was expected to toe the line. I remember that Citizens' Council sticker on our front door. My parents reflected the ethos of racism to the extent that when son Buddy was about four, he was able to sequester himself with the only phone in their house to let me know that 'Weese and D were anti-Negro.' That's when I began to look for ways to get the hell out of there."

My experience differed. The confrontation with my mother forever throbs in my heart, though my mind has relinquished the exact words. It occurred just after one of my transformative experiences. In April 1964, my influential high school teacher Mary Brooks (she taught me to think; Mrs. Eunice Hart taught me to write) took a group of us to historic Woodworth Chapel at Tougaloo College to hear Joan Baez sing. (My friend and fellow columnist Mac Gordon, another former weekly newspaper editor, wrote about a similar Baez performance he'd snuck off to in McComb.) What prompted the subsequent row over racism with Mama I do not recall. What I do remember, vividly, was asking how she could so despise Black people when she had trusted and depended upon our Black housekeeper, Willie Mae Pierce, to essentially raise my sister, brother, and me. Her response was to paint May May (our name for her) as an immoral lowlife. I was astounded at both the words and the vitriol. We loved May May like a member of the family (though not her long switches). Encountering that shadow on my mother's soul awakened me to cultural hatred. I had been too absorbed in my own adolescent shadows—inferiority complex, shyness, scrawniness, and envy of those with money and position. Somehow, that dark southern chain never shackled me.

Decades later I wondered how I'd escaped. My mother, an only child, came from privilege before things turned upside down and turned her bitter in a culture run through with bitter shadows. My father, on the other hand, who made his way with only a high school degree and army training and suffered through two devastating midcareer permanent layoffs, remained a cheerful, giving spirit in a culture also peppered with generosity and hospitality. The chain fettered her, not him. Why does cultural hatred infect some descendants but not others? Friedrich Nietzsche contended that love and hate are learned—some are taught by others to hate while some are not. Saint Augustine contended that some souls are more receptive to divine revelation of the truth than others.

By 2023, more and more Mississippians had been born and raised unfettered from the old chain (thankfully including my wife and children). The change in culture with regard to race was night and day, if a shadow-strewn day. For the most part, hateful utterances were seldom heard, interracial marriages occurred without incident, and Black and white mixed in peace without fear in workplaces, public venues, civic clubs, universities and colleges, many schools, and some churches. I wrote about these changes.

SACRIFICIAL, PERSEVERING LEADERS GAIN GROUND IN RELUCTANT MISSISSIPPI

July 11, 2020

These are still "times that try men's souls," Mr. Paine, but not as they did in your time.

When you penned these famous words in your pamphlet "The Crisis," the passionate issue was freedom from English tyranny. "Tyranny, like hell, is not easily conquered," you wrote, as you belittled the "summer soldier" and "sunshine patriot" who "shrink from the service of their country."

Not all agreed and heeded your words, but enough people did that independence was won and the United States born.

Today, the passionate issue is freedom from the tyranny of racism. Not all agree, but enough do that change, at long last, is spreading across America (and Mississippi). Racism, like tyranny and hell, is not easily conquered. And the enemy is not a wayward king on a distant island, but our own wayward brothers and sisters.

As American independence did not come quickly or easily, American unprejudiceness will not, either. The last 150 years have shown us that this change will take much longer.

As in Thomas Paine's time, winning takes the sacrifices and perseverance of many patriots. We have already seen that in oh-so-reluctant-to-change Mississippi from Black martyrs of the civil rights movement like Medgar Evers, the Reverend George Lee, Herbert Lee, Vernon Dahmer, and Wharlest Jackson; from thousands of Black Americans shot and lynched over the years, often for no more reason than the color of their skin; from whites standing up to racism being ostracized, run out of town, or having their businesses boycotted; and from white politicians thrashed at the polls because they were perceived as soft on race.

Federal actions in the 1960s could force change quickly on Mississippi, but not in prevailing white attitudes. But change they have as leaders, Black and white, persevered. By the late 1970s, white politicians with "moderate" views on race could get elected, such as William Winter as governor in 1979, and conservative House Speaker Buddie Newman in 1977 could appoint Robert Clark, the House's first African American member (elected in 1967), as the first Black committee chairman. By 1985, Gov. Bill Allain could appoint Reuben Anderson, the first Black Ole Miss law school graduate in 1967, as the first Black justice on the Mississippi Supreme Court.

In the late 1990s, more white leaders felt able to join William Winter as champions of "racial reconciliation," such as former federal judge and conservative Republican leader Charles Pickering. Chancellor Robert Khayat could ban the rebel flag and Dixie at Ole Miss and establish the William Winter Institute for Racial Reconciliation.

Still, racism in Mississippi persisted, though more in hearts and minds than the public arena; for instance, in 2001, 64 percent of voters chose to retain the state flag bearing the controversial Confederate battle flag.

When House Speaker Philip Gunn, a conservative Republican, courageously pushed changing the flag to the forefront this year, you could see the issue still trying the souls of many white legislators. But most did not shrink and, so, struck a major blow against the tyranny of racism, a remarkable win for sacrificial, persevering leadership in reluctant Mississippi.

"Let your light shine before others, that they may see your good deeds and glorify your Father in heaven." —Matthew 5:16

Despite these gains, great public divides remained in politics, wealth, and school choice. Most Republicans were white. Most Blacks were Democrats. All statewide elected officials and over 70 percent of those in the legislature lived in white households. Most of the people impacted by poverty and other issues holding Mississippi to the bottom lived in Black households. Most wealthy Mississippians, business owners, bank executives, physicians, and plant managers were white. Most prison inmates were Black. Median income for white households in Mississippi in 2021 was $62,953, but for Black households it was

$34,688. Both increased by 16 percent from 1999, but the gap widened at a faster rate, from $14,116 to $25,533. Whites still tended to flee whenever the Black population surged in neighborhoods and communities, causing many schools to resegregate. Most poor, struggling schools were majority Black.

Two vestiges of Faulkner's curse persisted. One was a simmering fear in some that the state's white population majority would be overtaken by nonwhites (a hope held by ardent Black separatists). That fear was stoked in Mississippi by new 2020 census data. It revealed that the state's white population had declined for the first time, down 48,500 since 2010. Interestingly, nonwhites composed a majority of the population for over a hundred years in Mississippi—from 1830 to 1950.

The other and most insidious vestige of Faulkner's curse remaining in Mississippi, despite heightened national tensions over Black Lives Matter, white supremacists, and such, was white indifference. In his landmark 1899 social studies text *The Philadelphia Negro*, W. E. B. Du Bois said with regard to racial inequities in health, "There have . . . been few other cases in the history of civilized peoples where human suffering has been viewed with such peculiar indifference." In 1965, the Reverend Dr. Martin Luther King Jr., in his commencement address for Oberlin College, lamented "the appalling silence and indifference" of good people with regard to racial injustice. Those on the receiving end believed that such indifference was continuing in twenty-first-century Mississippi. "Mississippi is not merely indifferent to poor people, our majority white, Republican, and yes, Christian legislators, seem to have contempt for poor people," contended writer Christopher Young in an August 2022 commentary in the *Mississippi Link*, an African American–owned newspaper in Jackson.

I criticized Republicans for failing to address this dilemma. My longtime friend and fellow Carmichael disciple Pete Perry argued I was too hard on his modern Republican Party. He said people he has served with on the Hinds County Republican Executive Committee and the State Republican Executive Committee would welcome greater Black participation. He believes that many Blacks simply do not want to join a conservative party that stands for cutting spending and reducing the size of government, but prefer a party that does the opposite. He admitted that the party's base did include "aginners" who retained racist leanings. Still, the tendency has been for Republicans in power to be indifferent or even antagonistic toward issues affecting those left out and left behind.

Indifference in Mississippi showed up in various arenas, including from jobs to hunger to prisons. I wrote about an example in 2021.

STATE INDIFFERENCE LEADS TO "HUNGRIEST COUNTY"

April 11, 2021

With unemployment decreasing, jobs growing, and state tax revenues up, rosy days lie ahead for Mississippi's economy. "The outlook for our economy is pretty optimistic for the state and for the nation," state economist Corey Miller told Mississippi Today.

But not for all parts of the state.

Consider Jefferson County in southwest Mississippi. No boom looming there. This rural, heavily Black county, population 6,990, looks to continue suffering persistently high unemployment. The unemployment rate for 2021 averages 16.3%, higher than last year; the highest average since 2014. The state averages 6.2%.

Job numbers continue to shrink, down every year since 2013, down 28.5% from 2010, and down 48% from 2000.The latest nonfarm employer-based jobs report (September 2020) showed 954 jobs in Jefferson County, with 539 of them state or local government jobs and only 415 private sector jobs. Notably, only thirty were goods-producing jobs (manufacturing, natural resources and mining, or construction).

The latest labor force participation rate was just 34.6%. The average annual wage was $34,080, which was 25% lower than the average state wage of $40,687.

The Clarion-Ledger revealed another dismal factoid last week. An October report by Feeding America identified Jefferson County as "the hungriest county in the U.S." Data showed the county as the only one in America with a 30% food insecurity rating. (Ratings based on poverty, unemployment, home ownership, disability prevalence, and cost of food index.)

Ding. Another new low rings up for Mississippi.

Hmmm.

Mississippi has eight counties, including Jefferson, that lost 10% or more of jobs from 2011 through 2019 and face double-digit unemployment today. All lost population over the past ten years. All have high poverty levels. And, yes, all have high food insecurity ratings. These counties are Holmes, Humphreys, Issaquena, Jefferson, Quitman, Sharkey, Sunflower, and Wilkinson.

That's 10% of Mississippi's eighty-two counties with wilting economies and growing human plight.

Now, these conditions did not occur overnight, but trends have worsened over the past decade. You might think that somewhere along the way the state would have adopted focused, well-staffed, and well-funded programs to turn things around.

Nope. And that's a sad story in itself.

Republicans in control of state government have shown little interest in providing more than limited economic development help for poor, heavily Democratic counties like these.

It's one thing to have access to programs, it's quite another to have professional help to implement programs. For the most part, job attraction and retention efforts and related development activities have been left up to each county. Left alone, counties with withering economies have little hope for a better future. The past decade proves the point.

Sad to imagine a state with leaders indifferent to the plight of struggling counties. Yet that appears to have been the case in Mississippi.

And leaves us with "the hungriest county in the U.S."

State leaders should be ashamed . . . and finally take action.

"And if you spend yourselves in behalf of the hungry and satisfy the needs of the oppressed, then your light will rise in the darkness, and your night will become like the noonday." —Isaiah 58:10

In 2022, the US Justice Department issued a fifty-nine-page report that pointed to prison officials' "deliberate indifference" to unsanitary conditions, gang outbreaks, violence, and low staffing levels at the State Penitentiary at Parchman, where 70 percent of inmates were

Black. The key finding was that Mississippi "routinely violates the constitutional rights of individuals incarcerated at Parchman by failing to protect them from violence and self-harm, denying them adequate mental health treatment, and subjecting them to prolonged periods in solitary confinement."

Over the years, the shadows cast by Faulkner's curse had largely diminished to indifference, particularly among state Republican leaders. But new energy poured into race-tainted politics in Mississippi when national GOP politicians began fuming and fulminating over Black Lives Matter and other so-called woke activities.

In arguing that race is central to Republican strategy for 2022 and beyond, Margaret Talev of Axios writes: "In an era when every topic seems to turn quickly to race, Republicans see this most divisive issue as either political necessity or an election-winner—including as it relates to voting laws, critical race theory, big-city crime, immigration and political correctness."

Critical race theory (CRT) is a forty-year-old theoretical approach to understanding what its legal-scholar authors see as persistent racial inequality and racism in America. It contends that racism has infested our legal, financial, and educational systems. Its new GOP critics, however, saw it as more than a scholarly theory. "Conservative lawmakers, commentators and parents have raised alarm that critical race theory is being used to teach children that they are racist, and that the U.S. is a racist country with irredeemable roots," wrote Isabella Zou of the *Texas Tribune* on June 22, 2021, after Texas governor Greg Abbott signed into law an anti-CRT bill.

As with many things concerning race, it did not matter what CRT really was, but how politicians and truth mangers 'splained it to us. At the 2021 Neshoba County Fair, Governor Tate Reeves and Speaker of the House Philip Gunn started 'splaining CRT's perils to Mississippians. During the 2022 legislative session, they got anti-CRT legislation passed, though there was little evidence of CRT in our schools.

Early in the 2023 campaign cycle, Reeves and State Senator Chris McDaniel began 'splaining the perils of "woke-ism," aligning their rhetoric to that of Florida governor Ron DeSantis. Later in 2023, State

Auditor Shad White, quoting both DeSantis and former president Donald Trump, began 'splaining the perils of diversity, equity, and inclusion (DEI) programs at our public universities. I wrote about this in 2023.

AUDITOR WHITE PLAYS DESANTIS, GOES AFTER UNIVERSITY DEI PROGRAMS

April 16, 2023
(excerpted)

Gov. Tate Reeves and the legislature having successfully stamped out the nonexistent critical race theory (CRT) programs in Mississippi schools, colleges, and universities, State Auditor Shad White has chosen another fake issue to tackle—our universities' diversity, equity, and inclusion (DEI) programs.

"After seeing Florida's review of DEI spending, we have decided to use the same model to review DEI spending at universities in Mississippi," Fletcher Freeman, a spokesperson for the auditor's office, told Mississippi Today.

Unlike CRT programs, DEI programs are alive and well in Mississippi universities. All eight public universities have DEI programs and policies. Most have websites promoting them.

Emphasis on DEI programs increased in Mississippi during the 1990s as universities faced court scrutiny as part of the [Supreme Court's] Ayers [desegregation] case. Both historically white and historically Black universities were under pressure to increase diversity and eliminate vestiges of segregation. That led to uniform admission standards and an *Ayers* settlement provision that encouraged historically Black universities to undertake "activities addressing other-race recruitment and retention."

Auditor White's Government Accountability Division required universities to research and submit comprehensive data on DEI programs. Yet, as with CRT, there has been no cause in Mississippi to spur such a request.

Given his following of Gov. DeSantis's anti-woke crusade, one can only wonder what Auditor White is up to. It looks to be a political fishing expedition, or in the current vernacular, a witch hunt.

In a published response (plus an emailed fundraising letter), White slammed not just my column but also me personally. "He belongs to a group I call the Aging White Liberals (AWLs)," he wrote. "AWLs often claim they were once Republicans to try to earn a bit of conservative credibility."

Weeks later, White released his 322-page report on university DEI spending. The *Magnolia Tribune* published a response by Mississippi State University president Mark Keenum. "We believe our ADI [Office of Access, Diversity, and Inclusion] program is fully compliant with all relevant current federal and state policies regarding such programs and that these expenditures represent a necessary and appropriate investment in Mississippi's future," he said. "That office is designed to increase higher education access and degree completion for underrepresented students, which is a necessity at Mississippi's leading research university," he continued. "Significantly, MSU enrolls a higher percentage of African Americans than any other university in the Southeastern Conference and a greater proportion of African Americans than any other historically white land-grant university in the nation. MSU's ADI program not only seeks to assist those students, but also empowers military veterans, first-generation students, former foster home students, students with a myriad of disabilities, Native American students, and others with a program goal of growing student success and degree attainment to help them lead more productive lives."

Reasoned voices like Dr. Keenum's and his university colleagues' appeared to hold little sway against the vitriolic voices calling for programs to be purged (and books banned).

Another notion that gained popularity among Republican politicians had roots in old, race-oriented views of welfare—think "welfare queens" and "shiftless Blacks." The diluted descendent notion was that able-bodied adults should have to work to receive Supplemental Nutrition Assistance Program (SNAP) and other such benefits. I wrote about the impracticality of this notion in rural Mississippi in a 2023 column.

PUTTING SNAP RECIPIENTS TO WORK MAY BE CHALLENGING

August 27, 2023

A major issue confronting state leaders is Mississippi's lowest-in-the-nation labor force participation rate—54.5% compared to the national average of 62.6%. A popular political notion is that there are many able-bodied adults drawing SNAP benefits who do not work, but should, and contribute to that low participation rate.

Let's overlay this on one of Mississippi's struggling rural counties.

Issaquena County, located just north of Vicksburg in the Mississippi Delta, suffers from high poverty, 21%; low average household income, $17,109; and population loss. Census data shows a 40% decline in population from 2000 to 2020 from 2,258 to 1,338. Estimates indicate population continues to fall, a trend other rural counties face.

The county's labor force participation rate is under 30% compared to the state's rate of 54.5%. The labor force participation rate in simple terms is the civilian labor force total divided by the population age sixteen and above.

Its civilian labor force totaled 320 according to Mississippi Department of Employment Security (MDES) data in July. Of that, 290 were employed and twenty were unemployed [*sic*]. Census data show the employment rate at 17.6% compared to 52.5% for the state.

Approximately 900 residents over the age of sixteen do not participate in the labor force. Some are older and retired, but age data suggest most are between the ages of twenty and sixty.

The most recent published SNAP numbers showed 218 recipients in Issaquena County. Some recipients may be already working, but a large portion are likely unemployed and not currently seeking employment.

But that does not necessarily mean they are employable.

Census data show that 42.5% of residents have one or more disabilities compared to the state rate of 18.1%. There are at least 429 adults with hearing, vision, cognitive, ambulatory, self-care, and/or independent living disabilities. Yet, only twenty adults receive Social Security disability payments.

Other data show 40.5% of the population age twenty-five and up without a high school degree or GED. Another 38% have only those education achievements.

Minimally educated, disabled adults do not constitute an attractive workforce. But if they want benefits, some may be forced to find jobs. Where would a hundred or so such residents find them?

The MDES Job Search tool shows only sixteen job openings within twenty-five miles of Mayersville, the county seat. Most are supervisor/manager or technical jobs.

Census data show sixteen county businesses and twelve government agencies with employees, and only two of the businesses employ more than twenty people. A high number of employed residents must commute thirty minutes or more to other counties for work.

Putting SNAP recipients to work and improving the labor force participation rate in places like Issaquena County will be a tough challenge.

"Do what is right." —Psalm 34:14

The rise of race-tainted politics undermined long-term gains made in race relations symbolized by adoption of the new Mississippi state flag. State leaders began to tilt at ideological windmills rather than grapple with Mississippi's real dilemmas. New shadows of Faulkner's curse emerged. Behaviors succored by both old and new shadows continued to perpetuate holes in the whole and thwart good government.

THE DOUBLE WHAMMY

Robert K. Greenleaf, author and founder of the Greenleaf Center for Servant Leadership, contended people are not stupid or evil. "The real enemy," he said, "is fuzzy thinking on the part of good, intelligent, vital people and their failure to lead and to follow servants as leaders. Too many settle for being critics and experts."

In Mississippi, the sister shadows of racism and hatred have not been the only flaws in our character. Parker Palmer, founder of the Center for Courage and Renewal, said: "In critical areas like politics, religion, business, and the mass media, too many leaders refuse to name and claim their shadows. With shadows that go unexamined and unchecked, they use power heedlessly in ways that harm countless people and undermine public trust in our major institutions."

Consider this perspective:

"We've had some city folks who had astonishing superiority complexes both in regard to the county and other parts of the city. They had all the answers already, no matter what the issue, and if they weren't going to be the big dogs, they weren't going to cooperate and be involved.

"We had Black and white peckerwoods both in the county and city, with their inferiority complexes and chips on their shoulders, looking for ways to be antagonistic no matter what the issue.

"And then we had some folks who were both profoundly self-important and profoundly insecure, thus having all the answers and being antagonistic to whatever and whoever came along."

That was my friend Tom Wacaster addressing a Lauderdale County leadership group in January 2000. Okay, that was Dr. C. Thompson Wacaster, the forward-looking champion of educational excellence and longtime executive director of the Phil Hardin Foundation in Meridian, daring to describe some of his kith and kin along with other acquaintances to motivate future leaders to get off their butts and do good.

He contended that the know-it-all self-important have no need for other ideas and options and that deeply insecure peckerwoods have no willingness to hear other ideas and options. He called the combination of the two a "double whammy." I knew and worked with some of the people Dr. Wacaster described. None were evil or stupid. Yet, as misinformed critics and misled experts, they could be, and often were, conspicuous obstacles to progress—in other words, effective aginners. I wrote about this issue in 2017.

BEWARE OF LEADERS WITH UNCHECKED SHADOWS

January 5, 2017

History tells us that when those who yield to their shadow selves choose leaders of their ilk, calamity, often war, follows.

Carl Jung labeled the dark side of self as "the shadow." His psychiatric research into personality found people to have inner shadows associated with feelings of guilt, fear, hate, anger, selfishness, etc.

Upon looking deeply into himself, C. S. Lewis said: "And there I found what appalled me; a zoo of lusts, a bedlam of ambitions, a nursery of fears, a harem of fondled hatreds. My name was legion."

Parker Palmer, founder of the Center for Courage and Renewal, teaches that we must know and confront our inner shadows to become whole or "authentic."

"In critical areas like politics, religion, business, and the mass media, too many leaders refuse to name and claim their shadows," says Palmer. "With shadows that go unexamined and unchecked, they use power heedlessly in ways that harm countless people and undermine public trust in our major institutions."

He was echoing Plato, who said, "In all of us, even in good men, there is a lawless wild-beast nature." Plato cautioned that tyrants begin as "protectors," then "the lion and serpent element in them disproportionately grows and gains strength."

How many times have we seen leaders pretend to virtuousness only to see their dark sides rear up to bring them down?

Then, there are those who manipulate our dark sides to gain power. They play to our fears, anger, and selfishness. As they rise to power, they breed more followers of like mind. "A leader," Palmer explained, "is someone with the power to project either shadow or light" and who "shapes the ethos in which others must live, an ethos as light-filled as heaven or as shadowy as hell."

In today's world, more and more leaders are rising up who play to the shadow selves of their people—Putin in Russia, Netanyahu in Israel, Erdoğan in Turkey, Sisi in Egypt, Duterte in the Philippines, Trump in the United States, and more on the rise in Europe.

We can see it at the state and local levels, too, where the politics of division and self-interest overwhelms the good of the whole.

When we allow our shadow selves to guide us, we open the doors of government to the "looters" and "moochers" that Ayn Rand wrote about. We set up the pathways to tyranny that Plato warned us about.

"Alexis de Tocqueville put it eloquently," said Ronald Reagan, quoting the historian in his famous "evil empire" speech—"Not until I went into the churches of America and heard her pulpits aflame with righteousness did I understand the greatness and the genius of America. America is good. And if America ever ceases to be good, America will cease to be great."

Our challenge, then, is to dwell more in the light than in the shadow and become like the teachers whose inner light stimulates young people to grow and flourish and like the pastors whose guiding light does the same for their congregations.

Leaders trying to change Mississippi for the better have had to face that double whammy as well as the residue from Faulkner's curse. Many have found it hopeless to try to pound common sense into hard heads filled with nonsense by truth managers. That has left us at the mercy of those who do not try, the self-important, insecure peckerwoods whose goodness gets tempted by hunger for power, recognition, influence, or wealth. These are the ones we too often elect or appoint to positions of leadership. I wrote about them in 2017.

SAVE US FROM DOOFUS-DRIVEN DEBACLES

July 20, 2017

"Doofus" is an intriguing and timely word. The *Oxford Living Dictionary* says it likely originated in North America in the 1960s and suggests it is either an alteration of the word "goofus" or from the Scottish word "doof," meaning dolt. The *Online Etymology Dictionary* says it is "probably related to doo-doo and goofus."

The definitions range from "a foolish or inept person" to "a slow-witted or stupid person" to "an incompetent and stupid, though well-meaning, person." Synonyms include dolt, idiot, nerd, fool, idiot, airhead, birdbrain, and boob.

The only doofus connection to doo-doo I could find was this, from Darrin Bell's Candorville comic strip (excuse the missing graphics): "Dear 'journalist,' I am offended by your biased hit-piece condemning so-called Fake News. You wrote '. . . some of these sites' main sources seem to be their rear ends.' Who are YOU to say what's fake and what's real? I don't know that your 'sources' are any more 'real' than my rear end. I know my rear end. I trust my rear end. You, on the other hand, are a total stranger to me."

No surprise that fake news and doofuses are related, but the rear end trust thing got me.

A blog called the Lunatic's Asylum had another take on doofuses and news. Speaking of "political pundits" in 2012, it said, "These people are put on the air because they have acquired, we're led to believe, a certain expertise, which is, sadly, all too obviously totally lacking. I cannot begin to count the number of times one of these professional pundits, paid attack dogs, campaign confederates, party hacks, the so-called strategists are trotted out to examine every possible detail of even the least interesting and least pressing subjects in minute detail, and to put a political 'spin' on it all. What's truly amazing, though, is that it's often the SAME doofuses showing up all over the same networks, one day uttering what they consider an undisputed fact, and the very next contradicting themselves without ever (a) seeming to notice, or (b) making an admission that they have changed a position or assertion. This is Orwell's Doublethink in action."

In his novel *Nineteen Eighty-Four*, author George Orwell defined "doublethink" as "the power of holding two contradictory beliefs in one's mind simultaneously, and accepting both of them. . . . To tell deliberate lies while genuinely believing in them, to forget any fact that has become inconvenient, and then, when it becomes necessary again, to draw it back from oblivion for just so long as it is needed."

Sounds so current, doesn't it?

In Orwell's novel, Big Brother was the tyrannical Party leader behind the doublethinkers. Today, the major political parties' powerful special interests play that role. And, like Orwell's Party, they primarily seek "power entirely for its own sake."

It is not that hard to detect all the doublethinking doofuses—the talking heads, the duped politicians, the ardent followers on the left and the right. The ultimate question is, will the vast majority of Americans join them, or will some commonsense coalition get off their rear ends and save us from doofus-driven debacles?

No such commonsense coalition had appeared by 2022, something I wrote about.

STATE FACING NONSENSE VS. COMMONSENSE CLIFFHANGER?

January 9, 2022

Listening to Gov. Tate Reeves and House Speaker Philip Gunn, the top issue for Mississippi's future is eliminating the personal income tax.

That's a popular political perspective.

Mississippi Economic Council president Scott Waller told legislators that no business leaders have voiced eliminating the income tax as a priority. He added that some fear it could have unintended consequences.

That's a frank business perspective.

Corey Miller, the state economist, said changes to state taxes are unlikely to have any significant impact on the state's economic growth, employment, or population.

That's an expert economic perspective.

Lt. Gov. Delbert Hosemann has urged caution, saying that eliminating 32% of the state's tax base should be thoroughly vetted.

That's a commonsense perspective

Hmmm.

All too often in Mississippi, politically popular nonsense overrides realistic common sense.

Here's more. The head of the Mississippi Center for Public Policy wrote an opinion piece recently addressing Mississippi's lack of growth and prosperity. He blamed it on "bad public policy."

No doubt true.

He then listed twelve policies his policy center is pushing for state leaders to adopt that would "elevate" Mississippi to a better future.

Hmmm.

Remember Blueprint Mississippi? That was the Mississippi Economic Council's business-led, rigorously researched planning process to establish policy priorities to make Mississippi more competitive with twelve neighboring states.

Interesting how little the two lists have in common.

Dare I say it again? All too often in Mississippi, politically popular nonsense overrides realistic common sense.

Into this setting come billions of extra dollars for the governor and Mississippi legislature to play with this year.

"The state has an extra $4.2 billion to spend," Mississippi Today reported last week. It comes from "federal largesse" for COVID-19 recovery, federal infrastructure funding, and increased state revenues driven by federal stimulus spending.

Most of it is one-time money, meaning it will not be available in the future to cover recurring expenses such as teacher pay raises and tax cuts.

Hosemann explained, "There will be many proposals to use one-time money on fleeting items." He said his hope is that leaders will focus instead on "generational change."

"Years from now, we want to be able to point to the positive difference this influx of resources has made in our state," he said.

Hmmm.

The interplay between politically popular nonsense and realistic common sense in our state capitol will have higher stakes than normal this year. Could be a cliffhanger.

"My son, do not let wisdom and understanding out of your sight, preserve sound judgment and discretion; then you will go on your way in safety, and your foot will not stumble." —Proverbs 3:21 & 23

In addition to competing nonsense and commonsense ideas, state leaders often exhibited schizophrenic behavior on issues. I have written about several examples. In 2019, I wrote about state leaders' concerns over federal overreach. The legislature had adopted a resolution for Mississippi to join thirteen other states calling for a convention of the states to amend the US constitution to "limit the power and jurisdiction of the federal government." The rationale, in part, was that "the federal government has invaded the legitimate roles of the states through the manipulative process of federal mandates." However, I wrote, the same legislature opposing federal overreach was guilty of the very same overreach with local governments. "Ask a mayor about home rule. Ask a supervisor about unfunded state mandates. Ask a school board member about policy flexibility. Indeed, state overreach into local affairs far exceeds federal overreach into state affairs."

I wrote about another example in 2019.

IT'S NOT SOCIALISM UNLESS WE SAY IT IS

June 10, 2019

Antidisestablishmentarianism.

Yes, it really is a word. Back in the day we thought we were something because we could spell what we thought to be the longest word in the dictionary. Didn't really know what it meant, but we had the spelling down.

It's one of the many "isms" of little popularity today in contrast to those that never fade, but persist. Racism, for example, is our persistent shadow in Mississippi.

Then there are those isms that ebb and flow. Back in popularity today are capitalism and socialism. Ebbing somewhat are their cousins, fascism, communism, and totalitarianism.

My favorite word architect, conservative columnist George Will, wrote recently about Republicans and socialism.

He said that Senate Republicans voting to revive the not-dead-after-all Export-Import Bank is an example of socialism. In so doing, he defined the essence of socialism as "government allocation of capital."

He claimed that the bank "exists to allocate credit by political criteria rather than the market's efficiency criterion." He lamented that only sixteen GOP senators "mean what they say when praising free markets and limited government."

Thirty-seven Republicans, now apparently neosocialists, voted for reviving the bank.

This starts to expose the hypocrisy in today's conservative consternation about socialism.

Will says Senate Republicans' Export-Import Bank vote "is a redundant reminder that the rhetorical discord between the parties exaggerates their actual differences."

Republicans tend to rant against socialism with regard to programs that benefit the poor and elderly such as welfare and Medicare, but stay quiet about it with regard to programs that benefit corporations and businesses, like the Export-Import Bank. Democrats tend to do the opposite.

Will calls this "politicizing the allocation of resources."

We see this at play in Mississippi. For example, our Republican leaders thwart expanding Medicaid to benefit the working poor, then jump all over providing financial benefits to corporations like Continental Tire.

This business example is widespread in Mississippi. It forms the foundation of our economic development programs. Capital is allocated to companies through tax rebates, tax credits, tax breaks, the federally funded Community Development Block Grant program, and the state-funded Mississippi Major Economic Impact Authority bond program and Small Municipal and Limited Population Counties grant program. All are among the fifty-three such programs listed on the MississippiWorks.org website.

We don't see conservative Republicans in Mississippi rail against socialism when a new, subsidized economic development project gets announced in their hometowns.

This headline of Will's column tells the story—"On This Policy, Republicans Are Socialists. They Just Don't Want You to Know."

The reality is, a complex democratic republic like ours needs a mix of capitalism and socialism to function. Whether it is the allocation of capital to areas of human need or to areas of employment need, both have a role. The extent and cost of those needs should be the discussion, not to go all in on unrestrained capitalism or socialism.

The ism that describes this is pragmatism. That great socialist Ronald Reagan practiced this in his advocacy for expanding the earned income tax credit to aid the working poor.

The ism that describes conservatives' current disingenuous position on socialism (see the 193 isms listed at https://ismbook.com/ism-list/) is "perspectivism." It holds that "judgments of truth and value depend on an individual's context or viewpoint."

In other words, "it's not socialism unless we say it is."

Such schizophrenic behavior has become a common technique used by truth managers. Whatever position attracts followers will be used, even though it may contradict a previously highlighted position. Stephen Covey, author of *The 7 Habits of Highly Effective People*, wrote about leadership changes that allow such messaging. His research on leadership in America found that we have moved from a cultural paradigm based on "character" to one based on "personality." The character paradigm embraces duty, responsibility, self-sacrifice, and virtue. The personality paradigm embraces selfishness, greed, pride, and self-righteousness. The one entails persistence, the other self-indulgence. "Self-centered indulgence, pride, and a lack of shame over sin are now emblems of the American lifestyle," wrote Billy Graham in 2012. "My heart aches for America and its deceived people."

A study Bible entitled *The Leadership Bible: Leadership Principles from God's Word* highlights what should be expected from our leaders. These highlights include traits such as character, courage, humility, integrity, self-discipline, wisdom, and obedience to God; skills such as accountability, communication, conflict management, empowerment, planning, problem solving, stewardship, team building, and systems thinking; and attributes such as healthy alliances, servant leadership, and encouragement.

Regrettably, more and more of us these days are influenced by personalities deemed leaders by social and political media rather than godly men and women in our communities.

INSANITY

"Insanity is doing the same thing over and over and expecting different results"—attributed to Albert Einstein.

Quite a number of former Mississippi leaders saw the administrative framework required by the state's 1890 constitution in large part responsible for the failure of government to move Mississippi forward. Thrust weak leaders into that matrix of innumerable agencies and commissions with overlapping functions and duplicating authorities, six constitutional officers (governor, lieutenant governor, secretary of state, attorney general, treasurer, and auditor) each with his or her own agenda, lack of executive budget authority, and no one with the power to implement a plan if one were developed, and failure could only follow. Former state treasurer Bill Cole described it as "an antiquated organizational structure that defies development of an agenda for action, that stifles policy coordination, and makes long-range planning nonexistent."

Time and again Mississippi leaders have tried to make this flawed system work, but have failed time and time again. Mississippi's longtime residence at the bottom of national rankings provides clear evidence of such insanity—if the system worked, rankings would move up from the bottom.

Actions to resolve funding problems at the Public Employees' Retirement System (PERS) provides another example of doing the same unworkable thing over and over. At the very end of his second term, Governor Haley Barbour threw out one last hardball. He saw that the funding path for PERS was "financially unsustainable" and pitched the idea that substantive changes were needed. He appointed a twelve-member study commission to recommend steps to align benefits with funding capacity. I served as a subcommittee chair and wrote part of the final commission report.

The report came just in time for the 2012 session of the legislature, the first year for Republicans to control both the House and the Senate. Phil Bryant was sworn in as governor, Tate Reeves as lieutenant governor, and Philip Gunn was elected speaker of the house, all Republicans. What did they do with the recommendations from Haley's PERS commission? Nothing. Not then. Not later.

As I wrote in a column on November 26, 2013, Lieutenant Governor Reeves actually said, "The fact that our pension funding levels are weak and getting weaker, that's a real issue. But heretofore, there has not been the political will to do anything about it." I continued to write about PERS' problems frequently. Here is an excerpt from 2016.

PERS' DEFICIT "MORTGAGE" BALLOONING, NOT SHRINKING

December 17, 2016
(Excerpted)

You know how a mortgage works, right? You make your monthly payments, and gradually your mortgage balance comes down.

Pat Robertson, executive director of the Mississippi Public Employees' Retirement System (PERS), tells legislators and retirees to think of PERS' massive $16.8 billion funding shortfall as a mortgage: "Having an unfunded liability (deficit) is analogous to having a mortgage and making mortgage payments faithfully every month."

Well, PERS' deficit "mortgage" does not work like yours and mine. Despite four years of payments, the balance has ballooned, not shrunk. And the number of years to pay off the mortgage has jumped from 30 to 40.6 years.

In October 2012, PERS increased public employer contributions to 15.75% of wages to start making those faithful mortgage payments on its then $14.5 billion deficit. Robertson assured all that this high rate would improve the funded liabilities ratio from 58% to 80% by 2042.

Four years later, the unfunded amount has risen from $14.5 billion to $16.8 billion, and the time to reach the 80% funding level target has moved out to 2053.

In other words, four years' worth of payments didn't lower the "mortgage" balance any. Instead, it increased by $2.3 billion, and the mortgage's term had to be extended, making it 40.6 years from its start in 2012.

So, PERS is out of compliance, again, with accounting standards.

To get in compliance without legislative action, PERS would have to increase employer contributions from 15.75% to 17.4% for thirty more years.

In an excellent analysis, blog site Jackson Jambalaya points to significant structural problems in concluding: "The numbers that should be getting smaller are getting larger while the numbers that should be getting larger are getting smaller. In other words, PERS is going in the wrong direction."

Key findings cited in the blog include:

"The ratio of active employees to retirees is getting worse as it declined from 2.3 active employees/retirees ten years ago to only 1.5 in 2016."

"The total amount of employee and employer contributions was $1.593 billion. However, PERS had to pay $2.48 billion to retirees. The deficit between the contributions and payments was $886.8 million."

"Investment income was only $217.8 million—not enough to cover the $886.8 million deficit. Thus, PERS had to dip into assets to pay benefits. The total assets of the PERS portfolio fell from $24.8 billion last year to $24.1 billion in 2016."

Legislators are the ones who need to find the political courage to fix PERS' ballooning deficit. An ever higher employer contribution rate is not the fix needed.

At the end of 2022, ten years after Haley questioned the viability of the retirement system, the PERS board voted to increase the employer contribution rate by another 5 percent to 22.4 percent. That was 10.4 percent higher than the level in 2011, when Haley appointed his study committee. The increase was due to take effect in October 2023, but legislative leadership pressured the PERS board to delay it. PERS pushed the date back to July 1, 2024. Then, in August 2023, it lowered the increase to 2 percent but projected that something similar would likely occur in coming years.

The recommended increase was the fourth time the board and its advisers contended an increase would solve PERS' funding shortfall. The earlier ones did not, and PERS' instability worsened. By 2022, the PERS deficit had surged to about $20 billion, from about $12 billion in 2011. Using this failed approach time and time again is a form of political insanity.

But the greater insanity came from state leaders' aggressively working to reduce the size of state government without planning for its impact on PERS. "I've reduced the size of government," said Lieutenant Governor Delbert Hosemann, a common boast among Republican leaders. Yet, nothing undermined PERS' financial stability more than the decreasing number of employees paying into the system. In 2011, a total of 161,676 employees were paying into PERS. In each succeeding year, that number dropped. By 2022, the number had dropped to 144,416. State agencies employed about 20 percent of all covered employees but accounted for 47 percent of the total decline.

The impact of the decline of employees paying in was magnified by strong growth in the number of retirees drawing out of the system. In 2011, a total of 83,115 retirees were drawing out. In each succeeding year, that number increased. By 2022, the number jumped to 114,462, a 38 percent increase.

GOOD SOULS AND MISSISSIPPI SCHIZOPHRENIA

Within months of each other in 1992, my father, William Bentley Crawford, and father-in-law, Dr. W. Richard Campbell, died. Both were beloved men in their communities, known for their servant hearts. Such highly emotional death periods can force your eyes inward to assess who you are and what your future holds in store. Following deep reflection and prayer, I decided to dedicate the remainder of my life to service in their honor. I just had to figure out how to do that and still support my family. In 1994, Dr. Bill Scaggs at Meridian Community College provided me with that opportunity.

"What confounds you most about our state?" Sid Salter asked in a 2002 interview for the *Clarion-Ledger* during my term as president of the College Board. "Two things," I replied; "our lingering love to hate and our sandbox mentality. Bitter the irony that evil seeds of hate and selfishness can grow in the same big hearts of people who reach out to help others in times of need. Mississippi schizophrenia—neighborliness and hate side by side."

Mississippi has been blessed with an abundance of good souls—the nurturers, the servant leaders, the difference makers in our schools, churches, and communities. People whom Glen Allan, Mississippi, native and *Eight Habits of the Heart* author Clifton Taulbert had in mind when he wrote: "Many of us remember a time when our lives and the success of our lives were the concerns of a great number of people, not just our primary families." People who step out of their shadows and lead in the light.

Most Mississippi community college leaders knew Dr. William F. "Bill" Scaggs because he taught, mentored, and worked with them. He passed on his experiences and servant-leadership ways by teaching for years in the community college leadership doctoral program at Mississippi State University, providing a quiet voice of wisdom many college presidents relied upon, and personally counseling and nurturing upcoming college leaders. His was also the wise and deliberate voice calmly mentoring local officials, legislators, educators, philanthropists, civic leaders, and agency heads. Bill taught me and others many valuable things, but what made him a truly extraordinary teacher, leader, and partner was not what he did but how he did it, with a spirit of love, kindness, forbearance, gentleness, self-control, goodness, peace, joy, and faithfulness, exemplifying the biblical "fruit of the Spirit." He was the epitome of what Robert K. Greenleaf called a servant-leader.

"If a gas line ruptured. Get Doodle. If the power went out. Get Doodle. If a family needed shelter. Get Doodle." Federal judge Mike Mills told me about the late Virgil "Doodle" Pate to describe how some good souls live their faith in good works. Mr. Pate, a lifelong Baptist, was a founder of the volunteer fire department, later fire chief for ten years, and Mike's indefatigable "assistant" Boy Scout master in rural Fulton, Itawamba County, Mississippi. "Doodle never missed a community gathering, whether PTA, political rally, cake sale, or revival," continued Mike. "Yet he never pushed himself to the forefront. He was a man of remarkable authenticity. Truly humble. He spent his life quietly urging everyone around him to be as good as they could be. He had a gift of making everyone else feel special, regardless of color or class in our little community. He could not conceive of being mean, rude, or selfish. He truly lived to serve others."

Mike's story reminded me of one of my childhood heroes, "Unca Bugs," I called him. He was actually William J. Mosby Jr., as congenial a man as there ever was. He owned and operated Mosby Drugs in Canton, a century-old family business there. But that was merely how he made his living. To the people of Canton and Madison County, Bubs Mosby was much more. He served a long, long span as Madison County's civil defense director. Fire victims knew Bubs well. He was always right there when something might be needed. He would immediately take it upon himself, personally, to make sure such victims got food, clothing, and shelter. When I was in high school, a farmer disappeared near the Barnett Reservoir. A number of us were there conducting an all-night search. Bubs got the search party out there, organized the search groups, and stayed all night and into the next morning when the man was found unharmed. If a drowning occurred anywhere in the county, Bubs would be there with his boat to help search. If anyone was in trouble or there was some "dirty" emergency work to be done, Bubs was there.

I learned about Oseola McCarty's extraordinary gift to the University of Southern Mississippi while serving on the College Board in 1995. She shocked the world when she, a quiet, modest, and little-known Black washerwoman, gave $150,000, most of her hard-earned life savings, to fund scholarships for worthy Black students needing financial help. Her story was one of hard work and perseverance. She was conceived in 1908 when her impoverished mother was raped in rural Wayne County, Mississippi. She also suffered with her family the decades of trials and tribulations experienced by other Black Mississippians. But her grandmother instilled in her a strong faith, work ethic, and contentment with her station in life. "Day after day, for most of her eighty-seven years, she took in bundles of dirty clothes and made them clean and neat for parties she never attended, weddings to which she was never invited, graduations she never saw," wrote Rick Bragg in a 1995 *New York Times* article. "She spent almost nothing, living in her old family home, cutting the toes out of shoes if they did not fit right, and binding her ragged Bible with Scotch tape to keep Corinthians from falling out."

Liz Cleveland and Lois McMurchy told me about Martha Allen, the executive director of Extra Table, a charity that stocks food pantries and soup kitchens across the state. "She illuminates every space with sincere warmth, has unlimited compassion, and is the most giving person I know," said Liz. "I have immense amounts of respect for my parents," Martha told Lois. "My parents taught servanthood from an early age. It is natural for me to think about others before myself. My parents paid my sister and me to pick up pecans so we would have money to buy gifts for a child that mom taught, whose family would not be able to afford Christmas gifts. We were reminded to be thankful and never to take what we had for granted." Miss Allen also cited her faith. "I know it is my duty as a professing Christian to show love and respect to everyone. My parents never allowed us to think we were better or worth more than the next human." Her father told her, "Baby, be kind to those on the way up so they will catch you on the way down."

I met Bernard "Joe" Hulin in June 2002 at a *7 Habits of Highly Effective People* workshop sponsored by The Montgomery Institute. "Little did I realize how significant an impact the training session would have on my personal and professional lives," he would say. "My life, or at bare minimum the manner in which I make decisions that affect my life, has indeed changed. I now experience a more intense feeling of an inner peace as a result of helping others." After completing a twenty-four-year career in the navy, Joe returned home to Preston in rural, poverty-stricken Kemper County. He developed Parents and Community Equals Educational Success, or PACES for short, an all-volunteer, community-based project that mentors Kemper County youth and provides them with the skills and knowledge they need to succeed in school and life. "The most satisfying experience of my efforts was the gleam of hope noticed in the eyes of the economically deprived children that we were able to help," he said.

I first met Congressman G. V. "Sonny" Montgomery in the spring of 1967. He showed up to tour the US Naval Academy. As a midshipman from his congressional district, I got to help show him around. Later that year after I transferred to the American University, Sonny's administrative assistant, Bob Montgomery, got me a part-time job in Representative John Bell Williams's office. However, I would hang around Sonny's office as much as I could because his female staff members were younger and prettier. Sonny sort of adopted me, giving me tasks like taking his clothes to the cleaners on Saturdays and inviting me to his condominium to watch the great Ole Miss versus Alabama game in 1969. Three decades later, it became my turn to help him out in our fight to save Naval Air Station Meridian. Over this period, Sonny taught me that public service driven by firm faith, positive relationships, patriotism, and perseverance was the key to good government. In 2000, with generous support from the Riley Foundation, I created The Montgomery Institute in his name and in honor of his servant-leadership legacy. I wrote about Sonny in 2010.

"ISLAND OF FELLOWSHIP" HOLDS OUT HOPE

December 30, 2010

A poignant scene at the 2006 memorial service for the late congressman G. V. "Sonny" Montgomery—two powerful men crying throughout the service. One was former president George H. W. Bush. The second was Missouri congressman Ike Skelton.

I recalled this moment when Congressman Gene Taylor promised he would vote for Skelton, chairman of the powerful House Armed Services Committee, for Speaker instead of Nancy Pelosi. Ironically, Skelton was swept out of office by the same anti–big government wave that had toppled Taylor.

Republican Bush and Democrat Skelton participated in one of Sonny's signal accomplishments—the Congressional Prayer Breakfast. "An island of fellowship in a congressional sea increasingly vexed by partisan rancor and bitterness" is how former Republican congressman and secretary of the army Pete Geren described the weekly bipartisan gatherings. "An oasis for the spirit," said former Republican congressman Ed Pease.

Tennessee congressman Zack Wamp, a Republican, described in 2001 how important relationships could form at these gatherings: "Each Thursday morning in the House of Representatives, I have the privilege of presiding over the weekly bipartisan Prayer Breakfast Group in the House. . . . It is a time where we come together in respect and love and full appreciation of each other. . . . Relationships are forged for life. I think of one relationship that was forged about thirty-five years ago in the House. A young congressman from Texas, named George Herbert Walker Bush, a Republican, came to be friends with a young congressman from the state of Mississippi, General Sonny Montgomery. To this very day, they are best of friends, and it all started with that weekly commitment to meet in the fellowship of the Holy Spirit."

"Sonny nurtured the prayer breakfast like the master gardener his garden," explained Geren, speaking at Sonny's memorial service. "It was his ministry to his colleagues in the House."

Because of his persevering leadership and ministry, members of the House gave Sonny a rare honor in May 2000. They named a room in the US Capitol for him. "We do not name rooms in this august building lightly or frequently," said

Minnesota congressman Jim Oberstar, a Democrat also defeated this year. Skelton, who joined Sonny so many times in support of veterans, was another friend, patriot, and prayer breakfast member who spoke up for Sonny.

Things change. The breakfast no longer occurs in Sonny's room. *CQ Roll Call* reported that partisanship has infected the gatherings. Still, many members come to seek that "island of fellowship." Mississippi congressman Gregg Harper is one who attends.

Given the nation's economic and fiscal plight, we should pray for more ministries like Sonny's that build relationships and foster bipartisan solutions to our problems. That's my prayer for the New Year.

Hard to believe with so many good souls that the great paradox of the South remained with us—those who can be so loving and giving to some yet so hateful and miserly to others. As Eudora Welty wrote in her classic *Delta Wedding*, "people are mostly layers of violence and tenderness wrapped like bulbs."

Ironically, no public body exhibited Mississippi schizophrenia more than the Mississippi legislature, where Sonny served for ten years as a state senator. On the one hand, most members were good-hearted people with intentions to do good for their people back home. On the other hand, their actions as a collective body could often be disheartening and uncaring, especially with regard to bottom-hugging issues. I wrote about this tendency in 2010.

BALCONIES AND BUDGETS

January 28, 2010

At heart, Mississippi leaders and legislators have good intentions. But, as Samuel Johnson and others taught, good intentions often beget more hellish than heavenly results.

Witness the fracas in Jackson over budget cuts. All know cuts must be made. All seek the best way. Yet, we see no consensus, just fuss and factionalism.

Makes you wonder if those involved ever step away, get up on the balcony, and observe everyone's behavior. Would such perspective give them new insight? Pull them together?

In *Leadership without Easy Answers*, Ron Heifetz says yes, it would. That is about the only way authentic leaders can externalize conflict and see paths to resolution when dealing with difficult problems, he says.

No problem in Mississippi. Our venerable State Capitol has balconies galore. But visitors to the balcony galleries in the House and Senate seldom walk away having seen resolution. And those peering over Rotunda balconies mostly see the oldest lobbyist in the world and his ilk plying their trade.

Rather than the broad perspective Heifetz suggests, our leaders tend to lock themselves into narrow perspectives. *Reframing Organizations* by Lee G. Bolman and Terrence E. Deal helps us understand. Their study of leaders found tendencies to see the world from one of four frames: factory, family, jungle, or temple. Factory folk tie solutions to structure and organization. Family folk tie solutions to human needs. For jungle folk, it's all about power. Temple folk use inspiration.

Take a moment and figure out the frames in which your favorite elected officials fit.

Many see government decision making as jungle stuff—power games. Now, power games are real and do have impact. But, as with most things, it's not that simple. Lasting solutions seldom result from crushing the opposition or reluctant compromise.

Lasting solutions to tough problems, say Bolman and Deal, occur when all four frames come together. Budget restructuring that takes into account human needs and reconciles power is still not enough. People must be inspired and motivated so they will earnestly implement solutions. Such solutions, while painful at the front end, lay a solid foundation for the future.

Many will tire of the power games in Jackson. That's when, if ever, factory and family forces will approach common ground. Will leaders then emerge who can inspire resolution?

If not, forget about the balconies at the State Capitol. Focus, instead, on the fact that it was built in 1903 on the site of the old state penitentiary, a site vexed with anger and shame. That will be a tolerable frame of mind as budget conflicts worsen into next year and good intentions rip asunder.

As noted earlier, but worth repeating, once Republicans took control of state government, the winds of power, money, and politics swirling through the Capitol swept new legislators up into power plays by the speaker of the house, the lieutenant governor, and committee chairs; thrust them into the reaches of the truth managers who had gained sway with leadership; and pushed them into the hands of special interests and lobbyists with their lucrative "campaign contributions." These power players dominated the legislative process to the extent that the legislature could hardly be called a deliberative body any longer. Only Lieutenant Governor Delbert Hosemann loosened control somewhat during his administration. Consequently, most legislators simply became minions of the ruling powers.

In contrast to the works of the good souls cited above, what did these powerful Republican leaders offer as their approach to alleviating Mississippi's bottom dwelling? Aligning with truth management organizations like the Mississippi Center for Public Policy, Governor Reeves and Speaker Gunn saw uncaring "starve-the-beast" budgeting and tax cuts as the best strategies to improve Mississippi.

So many good-hearted people in a state governed by hard-hearted policies—Mississippi schizophrenia at its finest.

MY SHADOWS

Journalism teaches you to find reality. Sometimes you find it by asking the right questions. Other times you find it by researching beyond the questions. Journalism taught me how government and communities work. It taught me to work long hours, to meet deadlines, and to be thorough (getting it wrong in print is a great teacher). Finally, it taught me that I wanted to do more than write about good things. I wanted to help make them happen.

At this point, I must admit to my own shadows and insanity. I confess my sinful nature and need to pray daily for forgiveness and guidance. Though once physically saved by placing my life in God's hands and another time glimpsing an angel sent to spare my mother's life until she could witness the birth of her first grandson, it took the Christian family at the First Presbyterian Church in Meridian years later to save me. In late 2019 I began adding Bible verses to my columns as a form of personal testimony. And while I escaped Faulkner's curse, I have struggled with Dr. Wacaster's double whammy. My adolescent shadows—inferiority complex, shyness, and envy of those with money and position—dimmed but never vanished. Early on they led me to make impulsive decisions, as evidenced by my "unique" career. Later, when I was a mature adult, they blessed me with a diffident, loner, contrarian nature, one suited to thinking, writing, and advising, but not with sociability or gregarious public leadership, and burdened me with periods of mild depression. This reality hit home in 1996 after my ego, inflamed with base closure success, led me to run for Congress. I ran surprisingly well, making the GOP runoff with Chip Pickering, but counted it a blessing to lose as I realized deep down my unsuitability for that job. My insanity reveals itself as I persist in writing columns urging change when none happens.

SUMMARY

Since Republicans took control of state government, Mississippi has remained at or near the bottom of numerous state rankings. Those in power appeared from indifferent to antagonistic toward dilemmas impacting those left out and left behind, resulting in hard-hearted policies in a state blessed with an abundance of good souls. Shadows of cultural hatred and too many self-important peckerwoods of both races helped spawn and sustain aginner sentiments that all too often dominate the Mississippi electorate. Meanwhile, insane political behavior survived as its own hole in the whole. Republican leaders tacking away from the good government course pushed by Gil Carmichael and Haley Barbour contributed to these negative trends.

Chapter Three

HIGHER EDUCATION

REORGANIZING UNIVERSITIES

"William S. Crawford, you are the undisputed winner of the title: Mississippi's most bigoted and rednecked man by the hordes of people who utterly despise you from: Alcorn State University, Jackson State University, and Mississippi Valley State University," read a note with a caricature of a Klansman that I received in 1995.

One story that shows the interplay of Faulkner's curse, the double whammy, and political insanity came from my efforts to reorganize higher education. I first gained notoriety on this issue in 1984. Representative Mike Mills of Aberdeen (now a federal district judge) and I determined to force the College Board to study university consolidation. We were concerned that the costs of higher education to taxpayers of Mississippi had been increasing rapidly despite decreasing enrollment. Plus, evidence had been accumulating that the excellence of said higher education was declining. All this had resulted in talk about the possible restructuring of colleges and universities. During the 1984 special session of the legislature, Mills and I passed an amendment that would hold up a $6 million appropriation unless the study got done. To avoid a rancorous floor fight in the Senate, Senators Cy Rosenblatt of Jackson and Stephen Hale of Moss Point pushed for a compromise. The two senators conferred with Mills, me, and the two Appropriations Committee chairmen, Senator Glen Deweese of Meridian and Representative Ed Perry of Oxford. Lieutenant Governor Brad Dye was also consulted.

Upon a promise by the College Board to conduct the study, we withdrew our amendment. In January 1985, the board delivered to the legislature a 177-page study performed by State Research Associates in Lexington, Kentucky. While the study was entitled "Restructuring Higher Education: Choices and Analysis for Mississippi," it became known as the "Foster Report" after the lead researcher, Dr. Jack Foster. It presented detailed research on the benefits and costs related to closing and/or consolidating institutions, programs, and off-campus centers. The study caused a furor among university constituents, so it was shelved.

In 1992, Governor Kirk Fordice appointed me to a twelve-year term on the College Board. That same year, the US Supreme Court remanded the *Ayers* higher education desegregation case to the US District Court for Northern Mississippi to identify and address any remaining "vestiges of segregation," including among potential vestiges the number of universities—three historically Black and five historically white. That put closure and consolidation back on the table but from a different perspective. Instead of fiscal prudence, the driving issue became desegregation.

In December 1992, the *Northeast Mississippi Daily Journal* asked me to write an op-ed piece related to the *Ayers* case. It was one of my more scholarly essays.

HAS MISSISSIPPI FORGOTTEN INDIVISIBILITY?

December 17, 1992

"Occidental College, like Thomas Jefferson's Monticello, surveys the world from high upon its hill. But Occidental gazes down upon an America more diverse, more fantastic, than in any Jefferson dream or nightmare.

"Jefferson feared that even a simple biracial America, whites and Blacks as equals, would not long endure. He advocated Black freedom but remained paralyzed by its implications." So begins Dennis Farley's penetrating article in the December 2 *Wall Street Journal*. He sees the multicultural student body at Occidental College as a test tube of American civilization. While the cultural variety at Occidental is greater than Mississippi's, the questions are the same. In Farley's following questions, simply substitute Mississippi for America:

"Can Americans live together? And assuming that, can they create something grander, more noble, than the sum of their disparate parts? Can Americans create an American civilization?"

The Occidental experiment "is colliding with an instinct embedded in the human heart—an instinct, ultimately, to cluster with one's own kind," says the writer. He cites *The Disuniting of America* author Arthur M. Schlesinger Jr.: "A cult of ethnicity has arisen . . . to denounce the idea of a melting pot, to challenge the concept of 'one people' and to protect, promote and perpetuate separate ethnic and racial communities."

It arises at a time when Iraqi pogroms, Yugoslavian "ethnic cleansing," and the Los Angeles riots—ultimate examples of ethnic separatism—are everyday news. It arises in a state where increasing Black "empowerment" and David Duke's presidential vote suggest fertile grounds for separatism.

Thus, the questions persist. Is America about divisions? Or is America about "transcending division"? Mississippi is deeply embroiled in this defining of America's multicultural future.

Our definition, like Occidental's, will result from how multicultural conflicts are resolved. (On my wall is a useful reminder on conflict resolution. For example, *procrastination* is lose/lose, *fight* is win/lose, and *consensus* is win/win.)

Last year, Lauderdale County's Black supervisor—the board president—passed a redistricting plan with one majority Black and two Black impact districts. His plan provided for consensus building with the opportunity to influence a majority vote of the board. Other Black leaders sued to create two 60% Black districts. They won. In a county just under 40% Black, they also created three very white districts.

In Jones County, community leaders merged city and county schools. Black leadership challenged the merger in court and won, effectively keeping city schools mostly Black. Warren County, however, was able to reach a consensus to merge its city and county schools.

In another county, a biracial task force looked at growing resegregation among schools. "Polarized schools and school systems mean a sense of separateness that will be destructive to the future welfare of our community," was the task force's conclusion. It is now searching for consensus solutions.

Lately, local multicultural conflict resolution has been overshadowed by the Ayers case. The US Supreme Court ruled that Mississippi's system of higher education remains illegally segregated. The Harvard Law Review critically describes the ruling as one that "establishes a virtually irrebuttable presumption that a system that contains historically Black institutions that remain predominantly Black is constitutionally suspect" and will likely "have to eliminate some, if not all, of their predominantly Black institutions."

The plaintiffs in the case and many other Black Mississippians are adamant that no historically Black institution should be closed or merged.

The College Board, in its court-ordered resolution to this multicultural conflict, attempted to be sensitive to ethnic heritage. Nonetheless, embodied in its plan, as indeed in the ruling of the court, is the doctrine that separate is not better, that America must be "one people, indivisible."

The Rev. Edwin King, a longtime civil rights activist, in testimony (unpublicized) before the Ayers lay advisory board, focused the issue:

"My own personal fear, shared by many friends, is that America is moving toward a two-tiered society. And that is our choice and struggle here in Mississippi. Will we move forward or will we try to perpetuate separatism and segregation, this time with more money and calling it 'separate but more equal'? We deceive only ourselves. I urge you members of this committee to strongly back our board and help rally public support for an end to discrimination and segregation."

Is Mississippi about divisions? Or transcending divisions?

It is clear to whom Thomas Jefferson looked for answers while defining this America we love. If we revisit Mark 3:24–27, John 13:34–35, and 1 Corinthians 13 from time to time, perhaps the proper answers will come to us. In the meantime, ponder these words the next time you say them: "one nation, under God, indivisible."

(Bill Crawford, a Meridian banker and former state legislator, is a member of the State College Board. This column was written at the *Daily Journal*'s invitation.)

After he read the piece, Dr. Rodney Foil, vice president at Mississippi State University, wrote me and said, "In relatively few words, you have captured the greatest challenge being faced by your generation of leadership in Mississippi."

In a confidential letter in February 1994 to my esteemed high school teacher Mary Brooks, a strong civil rights advocate, I described how I had developed my perspective and approach to closures and mergers this time around.

Dear Mary,

What a nice surprise to see you and Dr. Brooks at the Hardy luncheon Friday. Both of you looked good. I hope all is well.

You laughed when I said I had been thinking of you. Yet, it was more true than you know. I wanted to write you about just that.

It was a time of enlightenment for me when this very different teacher showed up to teach us American history at Canton High School. Of course, that's a very impressionable time in anyone's life. Of course, those were heady days in America . . . days of change, of idealism. But what implanted itself on my psyche was a direct result of you, both your teaching and your example.

I have trouble putting it in words. I suppose you could call it the birth of social consciousness. It was learning new ways to consider ideas. You were the first teacher outside of math and science to challenge us to reason. Most other social science classes centered on learning. There is a chasm between learning and reasoning.

You can imagine the impact of a call to reason in the midst of such racial bigotry and hatred on a psyche striving to find its identity. If people have destinies, then this changed mine.

Rather than pursue areas where tests showed my greatest aptitude lay (engineering, math, science), I groped for something more. I attended the US Naval Academy because it was away from home and free. I left after two years to attend the American University's School of International Service. While there I had the opportunity to work on Capitol Hill as an aide to Rep. Charlie Griffin. I found the Hill more fascinating than school, but more frustrating because of the continued racial posturing.

A wreck brought me home. I sought a Millsaps political science degree, but John Quincy Adams refused to credit my international relations courses toward his core curriculum. For forty less hours, I got a math degree. My attention, however, was in other areas.

I had found myself a job working for the *Clarion-Ledger*. I thought that reporting on events would be tantamount to changing things myself. For surely, history has been shaped as much by its accounts as its events. For almost ten years I worked as a journalist. One of the first stories I covered was the riot at Jackson State. Over my career, I interviewed KKK terrorist Tommy Tarrants; suffered threats for writing about Black political participation as editor of the *Tunica Times-Democrat*; and won editorial awards for challenging corrupt government practices in Tallahatchie County. But along the way, I found that reporting on events . . . even when those reports made the events more meaningful . . . was not enough.

I got involved with Gil Carmichael. His challenge to Jim Eastland in 1972 fit my image of the type of reform needed in Mississippi. So, in 1975 I talked Gil into hiring me. I worked through that campaign and so became involved in the Republican Party. Twice I served on the State Executive Committee. I held numerous positions in state and national campaigns. Along with Columbus lawyer Wil Colom, I participated in activities that led to the first Black members of the state committee. But again I found that trying to help others do things was not enough.

After working in Gil's 1979 campaign, I decided a career change was in order. Politics and journalism had resulted in minimal income. I had thoughts of marriage. So, I talked myself into a job at Bank of Meridian. I found I had financial and administrative abilities and rose to the number two spot in the bank. Along the way, I tried out politics for myself. In 1983 I was elected as a Republican to the Mississippi House of Representatives. As a reformer I helped Bill Allain with his government reorganization efforts, participated in the historic uprising that unseated Speaker Buddie Newman, and found myself becoming a major force in pushing higher education to reform itself (I was the instigator of the effort that resulted in the 1986 "Foster Report" on higher education that directly led to the creation of the position of commissioner).

Two children and growing job responsibilities led me to give up my House seat. After upsetting my Republican friends by supporting Ray Mabus for governor in 1987, I found myself devoting my energies to community development. I have held top positions in economic development, chamber, and numerous other civic organizations. Then, in 1991, I got to do something very fulfilling.

That was the year I headed Meridian's effort to save its navy base. I discovered a new talent . . . the ability to mold, focus, and lead a broad-based team. The success of that effort led to an even more meaningful experience in 1993. This time, Meridian was not defending itself from attacks by another base, but was recommended for closure by the navy. Given little chance, our team was once again successful.

Between these two experiences, my father died. You never knew my father. He had only a high school education and meagre income. It took me many years to learn that those things were meaningless. Despite life's burdens, he was a helper, a giver, a friend. To honor him, I made a vow to do more to help others.

It was a surprise to me to get Gov. Kirk Fordice's last appointment to the College Board. Because I had supported Mabus in 1987, I was somewhat of an outcast from the Republican Party. The navy base fight had kept me out of gubernatorial politics in 1991. Nonetheless, Fordice appointed me.

Immediately thereafter, the US Supreme Court rendered its decision on the *Ayers* case. Throughout the process that has ensued, I have agonized over what actions should be taken. The court decision clearly points toward desegregation with a goal of eliminating the racial identifiability of schools. The plaintiffs' submissions do not point in a clear direction but clearly would have the result of creating separate but more equal historically Black institutions while significantly altering, some say destroying, the better-integrated historically white institutions. Many in the state would have the historically Black institutions closed.

I am prohibited by the federal magistrate from discussing current settlement talks. However, I believe I can say the following. I believe we are at a crossroads in Mississippi. I believe this settlement opportunity is the most important task I will work on in my lifetime. There must be a way to assuage Black pride, advance racial diversity, and preserve quality in higher education. I have found myself in a position of leadership on the board and am dedicating myself to this task day and night.

I chanced to talk with Dr. [Adib] Shakir about Tougaloo College two weeks ago. It made me remember that high school night Mike and I snuck up to Jackson to join you, Brownie, and one of your son's girlfriends at the Joan Baez concert at Tougaloo. That made me reminisce about the impact you have had on my life.

It may be that nothing will come of my current efforts. Yet, I wanted Mary Brooks, the teacher, to know that her hand is there in these potentially historic efforts; that it has reached there over the years in a way and in a vehicle she would have never suspected.

Thank you.

The summer of 1994 found the College Board back in federal court presenting a plan to merge Mississippi Valley State University and Delta State into a new Delta Valley institution, and Mississippi University for Women into Mississippi State. I was called upon to be the board's lead witness. My testimony occurred on June 23, 1994. It was one of the most arduous undertakings of my career. First, I presented the board's plan under questioning by lead attorney Bill Goodman. Next, I was questioned by US Justice Department attorney Laverne Younger, and then by plaintiff's attorney Alvin Chambliss. In a letter to me dated June 25, 1994, Mr. Goodman wrote the following. "This is to again express my personal thanks for your taking the time and energy to prepare for and present the board's proposal. You did a job which, in my judgment, could not have been effectively done by anyone else. All of those working so hard in public education are indebted to you. I regret that the politics and publicity surrounding all this puts such an unfair strain on every spokesman. I cannot help that. But it makes me appreciate your contribution all the more."

The public perception was different. Sid Salter wrote about that.

CRAWFORD MADE GOAT IN *AYERS* CASE

By Sid Salter
July 1994

Most Mississippians know by now what the *Ayers* case is costing Mississippi in terms of progress in race relations—with good will between Blacks and whites in Mississippi eroding daily as this divisive issue unfolds. I cannot remember racial polarization being greater in this state at any time since my childhood in the early 1960s.

Now comes an Associated Press examination of the *Ayers* case from a purely financial standpoint, which points out that millions upon millions of dollars are being spent engaging in what has now become a political bloodsport. And there's no end in sight. Over the life of the nineteen-year-old lawsuit, estimates of legal costs and administrative costs approach a total of approximately $5 million. Some involved in the case think that estimate is light.

The Jackson law firm of Watkins and Eager has earned more than $2.2 million in legal fees working on the Ayers case since 1981. Plaintiffs' lawyer Alvin Chambliss estimated that legal costs for the Justice Department and the plaintiffs over the past two years exceed $1 million. The State College Board has budgeted $800,000 for trial costs alone.

In recent days, College Board member Bill Crawford has been made the whipping boy in this case by the plaintiffs and by some members of the media in this state who have established keeping all eight Mississippi universities open as part of their agenda.

By quoting Crawford's courtroom testimony out of context, he has been unfairly painted as the author of a College Board philosophy of "sharing the pain" of Ayers by closing Mississippi University for Women to offset the closing of Mississippi Valley State University.

MUW alumnae quickly began raking Crawford over the coals, as did MVSU partisans. The fact that eight out of twelve College Board members—a including both Black and female members—supported the April 1994 merger/closure proposal got lost in the political shuffle.

But what those MUW supporters—along with those carrying the water of all the individual institutions—fail to recognize is the simple fact that while it's easy to be opposed to closure, merger, or other extreme measures that may be part of the process of increasing desegregation of the state's higher education system, the hard part is admitting that it will be virtually impossible for all eight institutions to escape a significant measure of "pain" Crawford alluded to in his testimony. *Ayers*, at its core, is about redividing the higher education pie in Mississippi. One institution can't suddenly get a larger slice without changing the portion that his neighbor had previously received.

What Crawford and people like him have finally found the courage to say publicly in Mississippi is that we as a people have never sufficiently supported the eight institutions we have in Mississippi and that in a state as poor as Mississippi it is counterproductive to engage in another two decades of expensive social engineering to achieve a more significant integration of the higher education system.

That Crawford and others have resisted the completely asinine call by the plaintiffs for an across-the-board reduction of admission standards in Mississippi higher education indicated to me that at least some of the present College Board membership isn't seeking an easy political peace at the expense of the future education of Mississippi young people.

What is missing from much of the debate generated in the wake of Crawford's testimony from "W" supporters is their vision of how *Ayers* should be settled. They sing a pretty good song past the refrain of "Save the 'W'" and "save the Valley" and "save the HBCUs" (historically Black colleges and universities), but what is the source of the millions of additional annual dollars that will be necessary? How much of the existing higher education system should be merged, closed, relocated, shifted, reassigned, or otherwise tampered with as part of this grand experiment?

Five million dollars would build a nice, new building somewhere in the Mississippi higher education system. Fund a significantly endowed chair or scholarship program. The College Board plan that closes Valley and the "W" isn't perfect, but it does present a frame of reference. The plaintiffs still have offered nothing in return, save the infamous call to reduce admission standards—which should be more insulting to Black Mississippians than any rhetoric generated during the nineteen-year life of the case.

Until "W" and Valley supporters in particular and the plaintiffs in general are willing to offer a solution to solving the *Ayers* riddle as an answer to the College Board's last offer, it would be nice for folks on that side of the argument to unceremoniously get off Bill Crawford's sore back.

We would wrangle in court for several more years until April 17, 2000, when Judge Neal Biggers designated US Representative Bennie Thompson as the lead plaintiff. Up until that time, there had been only lawyers with whom to negotiate. Also, University of Mississippi chancellor Robert Khayat and Mississippi State University president Malcolm Portera approached board members about making a new attempt to settle the case. Both said the never-ending injection of race into nearly every board decision and legislative request was harmful and needed to stop. Our legal counsel believed the legal case was nearing an end, but Khayat and Portera were convinced only a settlement would end the litigation and compliance activities draining education resources and eliminate strained relations among university constituents and public officials.

It became clear that the board was ready to move in a new direction. The question was what it would take to get the plaintiffs to settle. Also, about this time Louisiana agreed to a $300 million settlement of its long-standing higher education desegregation case. It was here that I earned the label of "architect" of the board's settlement offer. Aware that the legislature would balk at a huge lump sum similar to Louisiana's, I devised a multiyear financial scheme to fund settlement activities. The key was to spread appropriated funds over a number of years. The total would be significant, but the annual impact would be reasonable. We ended up with appropriations for new and enhanced programs at Alcorn State, Jackson State, and Mississippi Valley State spread over seventeen years for a total of $245,880,000, and endowment contributions for each spread over fourteen years for a total of $70 million. Bonded capital improvements were spread over five years for a total of $75 million. A private endowment effort hoped to raise $35 million. With other odds and ends, the total cost amounted to $503 million.

In addition to money, the board also had to devise a plan that would accomplish what the US Supreme Court ordered, elimination of the remaining vestiges of segregation in Mississippi higher education, particularly regarding admission standards, program duplication, and mission statements. So, the resulting plan included a summer developmental program, new and enhanced academic programs at ASU,

JSU, and MVSU, uniform admission standards, designation of JSU as a comprehensive university along with Mississippi State, the University of Mississippi, and the University of Southern Mississippi, following through with remedial decree commitments, and more.

With support from Governor Ronnie Musgrove and Attorney General Mike Moore, the College Board entered settlement negotiations. Key participants were Jackson attorney and former Supreme Court justice Reuben Anderson, who served as the convener; plaintiff representative Congressman Bennie Thompson and his attorneys, led by Isaac Byrd (longtime plaintiff attorney Alvin Chambliss refused to participate); John R. Moore for the US Department of Justice; Governor Musgrove; Attorney General Moore; board attorney Paul Stephenson; Institutions of Higher Learning (IHL) executive director Dr. Tom Layzell; College Board president Carl Nicholson; board member Dr. D. E. Magee; and me, the "architect" and board vice president.

My notes show that Anderson opened the meeting and praised participants on both sides, saying, "Governor, we're going to read in the *Clarion-Ledger* that this case is settled." Musgrove called it "historic," adding, "We don't have enough time, energy, or resources to constantly fight." Byrd opened by calling the board proposal "shameful," then listed issues important to plaintiffs, including a demand that Veterans Memorial Stadium be transferred to JSU. Thompson argued for enhancing the historically Black universities, particularly JSU. Moore urged us to be "innovative and creative" and give our best efforts to settle, adding, "It will be good for everybody to settle this." Stephenson said the board had been out front with settlement as its number one priority and was determined to end the controversy.

A final settlement was agreed to by the participating parties, but it was not finalized in 2000 as hoped. First, the District Court required a process including a fairness hearing to approve the settlement. That delayed formal signing of the settlement agreement until March 29, 2001. Then, Chambliss led a rump group of plaintiffs to oppose the settlement in court. It was not until 2004 that his final appeal was denied and implementation could begin.

That delay was costly. I wrote about it in 2009.

POOR TIMING AND PERFORMANCE DOOM *AYERS* PRIVATE ENDOWMENT

October 29, 2009

During my extinguished [*sic*] career as an influencer of higher education policy, I was a goad for change—mostly tied to university closure, merger, and *Ayers*.

One of those *Ayers* things is back . . . my notion to provide endowments to historically Black Jackson State, Alcorn State, and Mississippi Valley State (HBCUs) and to link access to such funds to a "diversity" trigger.

During the 1990s, the impact of *Ayers* on the College Board was overwhelming. The 1992 Supreme Court decision, 1994 trial, appeals into 1998, and ongoing claims and counterclaims fostered an environment wherein all issues migrated to race. While the board, commissioner, and lawyers labored through litigation rooted in history, two university presidents looked to the future. MSU president Mack Portera and Ole Miss chancellor Robert Khayat told board and state political leaders that it was time to move beyond *Ayers*; that the image and reality of racial divisiveness were hurting all universities.

From this grew the impetus to settle.

Settlement had to align with prior court rulings to be approved by US District Judge Neal Biggers. Anything contributing to "separate but equal" would be denied.

My endowment notion came from three factors: (1) Growing diversity at historically white institutions reduced prospects for single-race institutions; (2) Incentives, not policy or programs, would be needed for HBCUs to attract other-race students; and (3) Plaintiffs cited lack of endowment funds as a key reason HBCUs could not compete for students.

So, to goad diversity, the board put a $70 million public endowment in the settlement. But a university could gain control of its share only by achieving a 10 percent threshold of other-race students.

As settlement neared, sentiment grew that Mississippi was about to move to the future, lifting itself from its horrid past. Corporate and private foundations were taking notice. From this euphoria crept the idea of enhancing the public endowment with a private fund.

Khayat and Portera believed private funds could be raised—and agreed to help upon final settlement of the case. So, another provision was added for the board to "undertake to establish a privately funded endowment" in the amount of $35 million on a "best efforts" basis.

With great expectations, all parties signed the settlement agreement on March 29, 2001. "It's time to move on," said the late Charles Young, longtime Black legislator from Meridian.

Protests and delays intervened. It was February 2002 before Judge Biggers approved the settlement; January 2004 before the Court of Appeals approved; and October 2004 before the Supreme Court denied a final appeal. By then, the luster was off. Interest in the private endowment had waned, and most public leadership involved, including Portera, had moved on. In this environment, Khayat raised $1 million.

Of the three HBCUs, only Alcorn State achieved the 10 percent other-race student threshold and got its endowment share. Today, however, Alcorn is back below 10 percent. The shares for JSU and MVSU remain unattained.

Now, come the Performance Evaluation and Expenditure Review (PEER) Committee and others wanting Commissioner Hank Bounds and the board to revive efforts to raise $34 million for the private endowment.

The delay between agreement and final settlement was unfortunate. But, the interim poor performance by the HBCUs in achieving diversity is telling. If the $70 million public endowment fund has not achieved diversity, how likely is it that any contributors will give millions to fund a private endowment for the same purpose?

As much as I own the idea and want it to work, even I cannot ask the commissioner and the board to do the impossible.

The hoped-for boost to Mississippi's national image evaporated, replaced with national media attention on Mississippi's continued racial dissention. Rather than a Mississippi moving away from its past, potential givers saw continued bickering by dissatisfied faculty and alumni of the historically Black universities and continued litigation by Chambliss's group. Big corporate and foundation givers lost interest, as did Khayat and Portera, who felt betrayed. By 2004, Portera had moved on and the dot.com bust eliminated most of Khayat's targeted contributors, although the chancellor did raise $1 million. Subsequent board efforts to raise funds found little support.

LOSING RON MASON

They had sustained, persistent, collaborative leadership that did its research, developed relevant and mutually beneficial strategies, gathered necessary resources, and pulled the segments of their communities together behind a common purpose. I cannot overemphasize the importance of sustained, persistent, and collaborative civic, business, and government leadership.

In late 2009, Jackson State University president Ron Mason faced catastrophic funding cuts and a proposal by Governor Haley Barbour to merge JSU with Alcorn State University and Mississippi Valley State University. He did what any intelligent university president should do. He put his rigorous thinking cap on. I wrote about that.

UH OH! AN IDEA WAS COMMITTED

February 4, 2010

Faced with catastrophic funding cuts for historically Black universities and the governor's call to merge them, Ron Mason did what any thoughtful university president should do. He put together ideas on what a merger of JSU, ASU, and MVSU might look like and how it could best work.

Then he dared to ask others to thoughtfully consider his ideas.

Boom! Mason's "idea" was leaked to the press.

Bam! An open-records request to JSU sought a copy of Mason's presentation and/or emails.

Kazaam! Mason is labeled a heretic, his "proposal" trashed, and legislators and College Board trustees reel from incited masses.

But Mason stuck by his intellectual integrity, saying that a merger would be preferable to "dying apart"; that, unified, the institutions could rise up like the fabled phoenix to better compete for higher education dollars.

A concept worth reflection, but with the media fanning the frenzy, thoughtful consideration, and the phoenix, flew out the window.

"I've looked at life from both sides now." That line from the Joni Mitchell classic resounds in my head as I ponder open meetings, records, and abuses. In the 1970s, I blasted supervisors for meeting and voting in secret, then hiding results until minutes were made public weeks or months later. I, like others, was ousted from public meetings because officials did not want the press in attendance. And so, I joined in the fight for the first open-meetings law in Mississippi.

Much progress was made and many abuses halted.

More recently, I served with executive agencies and faced legal, personnel, and management issues best handled out of the public spotlight. The open-meetings law properly provides exceptions for such, balancing the public's right to know with officials' need to discuss some issues privately and third parties' rights to confidentiality. While some officials continue to abuse the law, some media abuse public officials for meeting "in secret" when in fact they meet in lawful, properly noticed, executive sessions.

The public records law was intended to give the public access to official records. The Mississippi Supreme Court reasonably broadened the law to cover "records of all public bodies of government."

Now comes the concept that all ideas put in writing by public officials, like Mason's ideas, are public records. It's one thing to troll computers to see if a misdeed was committed. It's quite another to troll them to see if an idea was committed.

When "openness" closes off reflection and stifles ideas, the pendulum has swung too far. Mason's extraordinary and insightful idea presentation had a ways to go before it became a "public record." I've looked at both sides now.

In April 2010, we lost an outstanding president when Ron was named president of the Southern University System in Louisiana. He later served as president of the University of the District of Columbia.

AYERS DIVERSIFICATION RESULTS

I am honored, and flabbergasted, that an august body like the Meridian Rotary Club would invite "lying Bill Crawford" to speak to them. That's what the policy director of the Mississippi Center for Public Policy called me, responding somewhat vigorously to my March 2019 column on government transparency.

During the heyday of segregation, zero percent of Black students attended historically white universities. In 1976, the ratio rose to 25 percent. By the mid-1990s, the ratio passed 40 percent. Trends showed that the three HCBUs were losing market share among Black students while failing to gain ground with other-race students. The *Ayers* settlement sought to make Mississippi's three historically Black universities more competitive by giving them programs, money, and scholarships to attract other-race students. However, many faculty, alums, and students at those institutions did not want that. Without broad, sustained support, the settlement could not work and did not.

By 2020, the ratio of Black students attending historically white universities hit 53 percent. Even with the money and programs provided by the settlement over seventeen years, historically Black universities were hardly more competitive for other-race students than in 2004. In 2020, only 499 white and 379 other-race students attended ASU, JSU, and MVSU together. In 2021, total enrollment at all three had fallen below their 2004 levels.

As with other major initiatives in Mississippi, over time leadership changed on the board, on the board staff, at the universities, and in state government. There should be little doubt that dwindling interest in the settlement's goals by subsequent governors, majorities in the House and Senate, College Board trustees and staff, and most university presidents also played a role in these outcomes. And similar to the Republican Party's failure to diversify to mitigate race-oriented politics, historically Black universities' failure to diversify sustained race as a taxing tension in higher-education decision making.

SUMMARY

All three commingled areas (Faulkner's curse, the double whammy, and political insanity) came into play in the failure to reorganize and diversify higher education in Mississippi—the racial overtones exhibited in the *Ayers* case, the blackballing of Ron Mason, and the perpetuation of a broken system. On a personal level, my grand hope that I could help Mississippi find a way to assuage Black pride, advance racial diversity, and preserve quality in higher education proved to be naïve.

Chapter Four

OTHER IMPACTS FROM BEHAVIORAL SHADOWS AND POLITICAL INSANITY

PUBLIC EDUCATION

My notion after working for Gil Carmichael was that "good leaders" would be visionaries able to take on tough, sometimes unpopular, challenges to make government keep its promises in a more efficient and effective manner. What are the promises of our state government? Public safety, good to great public schools, functioning public infrastructure (roads, bridges, levees, etc.), and rational regulations are high on the list.

No hole in the whole exhibited our behavioral shadows, political insanity, and schizophrenia more than the legislature's unwillingness to provide the means for a good education to all children.

The issues facing public education became personal to me through a Ford Foundation initiative in Meridian when I served as vice president for community and business development at Meridian Community College (MCC). In 1994, the foundation decided to invest in a national demonstration program to determine if rural community colleges in the nation's most economically distressed regions could lead their people and communities toward prosperity. In 1996, MCC was selected to participate. A forty-seven-member community team rigorously researched dilemmas impacting community prosperity, then developed strategies to address nine critical areas, most dealing with public education: (1) teen pregnancies, (2) lagging brain development in at-risk children, (3) issues at private day care centers and Head Start, (4) children unready for kindergarten, (5) reading challenges in grades 1 through 3, (6) math and science challenges in higher grades, (7) teacher quality and professional development, (8) weak college developmental education, (9) an unskilled workforce, and (10) weak applied math skills in the workforce.

When helping recruit those forty-seven team members, I told them, "I don't know about you, but as a lifelong Mississippian I'm tired of being left behind. I'm tired of Meridian, Lauderdale County, and East Mississippi being left behind and left out. I want something better for my children. I want to face the enemy and fight. I want to make a difference. I want to do something that counts."

Good to great schools that provide quality education serve as the foundations for competitive workforces, strong economies, and good to great communities. Bad to weak schools do not. Yet, race and related peckerwood attitudes have long undermined public schools and quality education in Mississippi. Dynamic consequences of those historical attitudes followed court-ordered public school desegregation in the 1960s. That led to white flight and an upsurge of private schools that continued into the 2020s. When they took control of the legislature, many Republicans began to criticize public schools and to push for school vouchers. Significantly, they also resisted adequate funding for public schools, greatly impacting schools in poorer communities. I wrote about that.

LEGISLATURE HAS FLUBBED RESPONSIBILITY FOR GOOD SCHOOLS

March 8, 2018

With all the noise about school funding, school choice, vouchers, and teacher shortages, perhaps a look at some fundamentals would be helpful.

Remember 2015? The Initiative 42 referendum to put full funding for the Mississippi Adequate Education Program (MAEP) in the state constitution? That initiative and the legislature's alternative both failed. So, Section 201 of the Mississippi constitution remains unchanged. It reads, "The Legislature shall, by general law, provide for the establishment, maintenance, and support of free public schools upon such conditions and limitations as the Legislature may prescribe."

That means it is our legislators' duty to provide us with free public schools, and it puts the onus on them to make our free schools good schools. The constitution gives them the power. They can draw and realign school districts, establish standards for administrators and teachers, set the school calendar, establish school policy and regulations, provide teacher pay, hold administrators accountable, and provide different types of schools, programs, and pay packages for challenged districts.

Instead, legislators have pushed much of the funding and responsibility to the local level. This lets legislators cut taxes, limit school funding, and pass blame for bad schools to local folks. According to the constitution, however, this is not local folks' job. Section 206 of the constitution says this about local effort: "Any county or separate school district may levy an additional tax, as prescribed by general law, to maintain its schools."

"May." The constitution says local effort is to be discretionary.

It is not. Both the MAEP, and the apparently dead Mississippi Uniform Per Student Funding Formula considered by the legislature this year, require local school districts to contribute up to 27 percent of the "base student cost." Legislators also expect school districts to provide most, often all, of the costs for school buildings and related facilities.

Meanwhile, the availability of teachers is fast declining. The Mississippi Department of Education reported a 92 percent decrease, from 7,620 in 2007 to 603 in 2017, in the number of applicants for teacher licenses. Given our low pay, deteriorating teaching environments, constant curricula changes, and never-ending school funding fights, no wonder fewer and fewer want to teach in Mississippi.

It's pretty clear the legislature has flubbed its responsibility to provide free and good public schools. We have too many low-performing schools and too many unable to attract and retain good teachers. It's no wonder parents in those school districts are frustrated. They feel locked into bad schools with no recourse for their children.

Rather than address the bad school problem, legislative leaders this year concocted a "school choice" plan to expand access to Education Scholarship Accounts (ESAs). Already available for students with special needs, the expanded version would have given vouchers to selected parents to send their children to private schools.

What a cop-out to legislators' constitutional responsibility to provide good schools for all children!

Parents living in school districts with low-performing schools or in districts struggling to attract and retain good teachers look to the legislature to fix your schools and pay teachers attractive salaries. Diverting dear school funds to vouchers for private schools is not the solution our constitution authorizes or envisions.

As noted, the 1890 constitution places responsibility for providing free schools directly on the legislature, but legislators shoved part of that burden onto local communities. As a result, better-off areas paid teachers extra and provided better facilities, yielding them better schools and better-performing students. That let legislators hold down state taxes but forced local governments to keep raising taxes to support their schools. MAEP, which passed in 1997 to guarantee "adequate" funding for all schools, was supposed to fix that problem. But the legislature could only find money to fully fund the state's share twice, in 2003 and 2008, yet found money to cut taxes time and again. (Note: the legislature appropriated full funding for 2009 and 2010, but midyear budget cuts reduced actual funds received; the legislature never did restore those cuts.) Also, the state provided millions of dollars in bonds to build and improve facilities at universities and community colleges, but little for public schools. That responsibility was mostly passed to local school districts.

Given the above-cited trends, it seemed schizophrenic in 2013 when Governor Phil Bryant and legislative leaders allowed a few positive ventures to develop. As they continued to deny full funding for MAEP, they enacted the Literacy-Based Promotion Act, known as the third grade gate, which provided intensive reading instruction and intervention in elementary schools. The program, modeled after Florida's program (established by good government conservative Governor Jeb Bush), halted social promotion and placed reading coaches in the most challenged elementary school classrooms. Over the next ten years, National Assessment of Educational Progress (NAEP) tests in fourth-grade reading began to show major improvement.

This success resulted in large part from the evidence-based science of reading approach promulgated by the Barksdale Reading Institute. The institute was founded by entrepreneur Jim Barksdale and his wife, Sally, with a $100 million contribution in 2000. In the summer of 2022, upon announcing the end of the institute's two decades of literacy work, CEO Kelly Butler said, "For over twenty-two years BRI has worked hand-in-hand with Mississippi's schools of education, public schools and pre-K programs, and thousands of dedicated teachers, and has played a critical role in the significant improvement in reading scores in the state. In 2000, Mississippi students ranked forty-ninth on fourth-grade reading scores as measured by the . . . NAEP. In 2019, Mississippi ranked twenty-sixth at the national average, and is among the top performers in accelerating growth for children in poverty and for children of color." In addition, the legislature funded efforts to improve high school graduation rates. By 2023, Mississippi's graduation rate hit 88.9 percent, the highest ever, and exceeded the national average of 86.5 percent. Both improvements received positive national press.

Also, in response to a growing teacher shortage, state leaders began to address low teacher pay, with a big one-time increase in 2022.

Then, in 2023, the legislature had one more chance to fully fund MAEP. The Senate unanimously passed a bill for full funding with a slight adjustment to the formula. However, the bill stalled in the House in the face of Speaker Philip Gunn's strong opposition. The Senate move did result in a special one-time increase in school funding of $100 million.

These lanterns of progress, however, did not light up the long, lingering shadows. In 2023, teacher concerns about safety, dilapidated facilities, and student behavior increased. The serious teacher shortage continued. And sustained student progress was still absent, something I wrote about.

DATA SEARCH FAILS TO REVEAL SUSTAINED STUDENT PROGRESS

June 11, 2023

Sometimes it's fun to rummage around in published data to see what you can find—or not find.

The recent article in the *New York Times* expounding progress by Mississippi students prompted my latest rummage. The third grade reading gate promulgated by Gov. Phil Bryant in 2013 was given much credit for marvelous improvements in NAEP scores by Mississippi fourth graders.

So how about ACT scores, I wondered? Are those early grade improvements sticking through high school? Also, with graduation rates up, are more Mississippi high school grads going to Mississippi public universities?

I delved into Mississippi Department of Education (MDE) data first. NAEP scores for fourth grade reading and math have jumped significantly since 2013. The ACT assessment is given during the junior year. A 2013 fourth grader would have been a junior in 2020. So, from 2020 through 2022, how much did ACT scores improve?

Nada.

Instead, the average composite ACT score trended down, from 17.6 to 17.4. So, too, did the average scores for the math and reading sections.

A look back at MDE information on NAEP scores showed that fourth grade gains hardly extended to eighth grade. Maybe we need an eighth grade gate, too.

The grad to university question got dicey. Nowhere could I find how many high school students graduate each year. I could find graduation percentages, which are up, but no numbers.

The closest to an actual number comes from multiplying the graduation rate times the four-year cohort used by the formula. For 2023, that would be 88.9% times 32,681 for 29,053. Add on 11% for private school graduates (the proportion of high school students attending private schools), and the number increases to 32,249.

The MDE website showed that 12% of the 2020 graduating class enrolled in a public Mississippi university. There was nothing more current. The percentage had ranged from 13% to 15% in pre-COVID years. Using 15%, the number of grads headed to our public universities would be about 4,800.

IHL data for fall 2022 showed that 15,405 freshmen enrolled (including holdovers). It also showed that 10,086 entering freshmen had ACT scores. Nonresident students made up 35.3% of total enrollment. Putting all that together suggests that a range of 3,560 to 5,437 entering freshmen were Mississippi high school graduates.

A third source should have had the answer, Mississippi Lifetracks, now an Accelerate Mississippi project. But it has not been updated in several years.

Yuck. Surely, more of our high school graduates attend our public universities?

As for my question, IHL data for 2017 to 2022 showed a relatively flat trend in the total number of freshmen each year. So, most likely the number of high school grads going to our public universities has not increased.

Not a great rummage, huh?

"For now we see in a mirror dimly." —1 Corinthians 13:12

In summary, the lack of consistent "adequate" funding left many schools struggling and the sustainability of the few gains in question.

Underfunded schools were not the only impediment to a good education for all children. Through 2013, Mississippi was the only state in the South with no publicly funded pre-K program for four-year-olds. In another schizophrenic move in 2013, the legislature passed the Early Learning Collaborative Act championed by Mississippi First, which began the buildup of state-funded pre-K education (another initiative influenced by the Barksdale Reading Institute). Senator Brice Wiggins helped lead the effort to gain a state commitment of $3 million to implement a demonstration pre-K project in 2014. Funding would increase gradually in subsequent years, reaching $24 million in FY 2023. Also in FY 2023, the legislature added $20 million for other early learning programs through public schools.

Missing, though, were resources needed to help disadvantaged and at-risk children from birth through age three. Dr. Cathy Grace, a forty-year advocate for early childhood interventions, provided Mississippi leaders with ample evidence that far more should be done. I wrote about that.

EARLY INTERVENTIONS COULD LIFT MISSISSIPPI OFF BOTTOM

December 23, 2017

What one thing could Mississippi do to have a more competitive workforce, a healthier population, more college graduates, fewer welfare mothers, better school performance, fewer special-needs children, and less drug usage, and pay for itself seven times over?

Improve cognitive development in at-risk children right from birth.

Sound too good to be true?

Science says otherwise. It has to do with neurotransmitter changes (such as serotonin and dopamine levels), synaptic pruning as a function of experience, gene activation associated with experience, and social transactions.

Say what?

Well, cognitive development deals with fundamental brain skills that enable children to think, read, learn, remember, and pay attention. From these fundamental skills, children develop their capacities to speak, understand, calculate, interact, and deal with complex systems.

Long-term research has now shown two things conclusively: (1) cognitive abilities get firmly set based on what happens to children during their first weeks and months after birth; and (2) targeted early interventions can make a profound difference.

This research has been the life work of Drs. Craig and Sharon Ramey. Leaders in Meridian and other communities will remember the early childhood development work the Rameys did in Mississippi in the 1990s. At that time, they were pioneering brain development research at the Civitan International Research Center at the University of Alabama at Birmingham. Now distinguished research scholars and practitioners at the Virginia Tech Carilion Research Institute, the Rameys have pulled together more than forty years of scientific research and tracking to irrefutably show that "cognitive disabilities can be prevented in early childhood."

They presented their findings last week at the first of a series of presentations sponsored by the University of Mississippi Graduate Center for the Study of Early Learning. Entitled "Investing in High-Quality Early Childhood Education Yields Economic Returns," the series will also feature Dr. James Heckman, Nobel Prize–winning economist at the University of Chicago, whose analysis shows the economic returns, and Dr. Pat Levitt, WM Keck Provost Professor of Neurogenetics at the Keck School of Medicine of the University of Southern California, whose research shows how genes and environment together influence typical and atypical brain development.

Significant impacts for early interventions include leveling the playing field in educational performance for at-risk children, improving their college going rates by 4 to 1, reducing their use of public assistance by 5 to 1, and improving their average earnings by 50 percent.

The cost-benefit analysis by Dr. Heckman of these targeted interventions showed a 7.3 to 1 return on investment by adulthood.

"The health, education, and well-being of children forecast the future of communities and states," said Dr. Craig Ramey. "If we don't get a significant sector of the population started early, it is hard to make a difference later."

So, Mississippi, do we want to grow a more productive workforce, smarter kids, and more college graduates while reducing welfare dependence, school retention, and special-needs demands? These are real outcomes that would lift Mississippi off the bottom of so many national rankings.

Science is telling us what to do and that the economic payback will be terrific. Are we in or out?

I learned about Dr. Craig Ramey's research in 1997 when Dr. Grace came to Meridian to help develop an early childhood plan as part of our Ford Foundation initiative. Later, she got Dr. Ramey himself to lead a prime-time TV forum to educate local citizens about brain development right from birth. Despite years and years of advocacy by Cathy and others, Mississippi lagged well behind neighboring states Alabama, Arkansas, and Louisiana for birth through age three interventions. It was not that state leaders lacked understanding about the benefits of such interventions. I wrote about that, too.

BRYANT TOLD EARLY INTERVENTION WITH DISADVANTAGED CHILDREN HAS HIGH ROI

February 10, 2018

Gov. Phil Bryant kicked off a recent seminar at the Civil Rights Museum auditorium featuring Nobel Prize–winning economist Dr. James Heckman. An expert in the economics of human development, Dr. Heckman spoke on "Making the Case for Investing in High-Quality Early Childhood Education in Mississippi." The Graduate Center for the Study of Early Learning at the University of Mississippi is hosting internationally known speakers to illustrate how investments in high-quality early childhood education yield a high rate of return. Dr. Heckman's research shows a 10% to 13% average return on investments (ROI) in high-quality programs for disadvantaged children age zero to three.

The governor, who met privately with Dr. Heckman after the event, spoke of his efforts to improve "the continuum of learning" for children. Citing the high volume of Mississippi children in daycare, he also noted that training programs at community colleges are working to upgrade the skills of daycare workers.

Dr. Heckman said the key to growing a skilled, flexible workforce in Mississippi is by building skills, and not just technical skills. He said research shows that developing "social and emotional skills" from birth to age three sets the stage for development of other skills. He added that "the family is the cornerstone of effective skill development."

"Conscientiousness, self-control, motivation, persistence, and sociability have far greater influence on full-time employment, lifetime wages, health, and family and social outcomes than IQ and cognitive skills," he said.

These are the soft skills employers yearn for in new hires.

Dr. Heckman said government should focus its limited dollars for early childhood interventions on children who will be most impacted. "The highest returns come from high-quality programs for disadvantaged children," he said. "Advantaged children have other resources often much better than those from public programs."

"Invest more in flourishing lives, not in correcting problems after they appear," he said. "Later remediation is largely ineffective."

Dr. Heckman was the second in the three seminar series the Graduate Center for the Study of Early Learning is presenting. Drs. Craig and Sharon Ramey, experts in early childhood brain development, made the first presentation in December. Dr. Pat Levitt, scientific director of the National Scientific Council on the Developing Child, will make the final presentation this week. Dr. Levitt will discuss his research showing how early life experiences influence social, emotional, and learning skills, and how these skills come together to help children succeed in the real world and how healthy brain architecture provides the resilience to deal with adversity experienced during the first years of life.

Interestingly, just days after the governor met with Dr. Heckman, the Mississippi Department of Human Services revealed that it had returned $13 million to the federal government because of the lack of state matching funds. These funds were for child care vouchers for low income families. The *Clarion-Ledger* reported that the governor's spokesman said, "Gov. Bryant fulfilled his statutory responsibility to balance the state's budget," and he "is appreciative of efforts by Department of Human Services leadership to continue fulfilling the agency's mission."

Hmmm.

What Mississippi needs and what we'll pay for don't always geehaw.

Failure to address early childhood interventions cascades into other areas besides schools. Consider this—over decades Mississippi leaders eagerly invested more and more resources into financial incentives and workforce training programs to attract high-paying jobs. But they only reluctantly invested in the need most indispensable to that goal—highly educated high school graduates. Meanwhile, those much sought-after higher-paying jobs began to require higher and higher levels of education.

"An educated and skilled pool of workers will be an absolute requirement [for Mississippi] to effectively participate in a more complex and technologically sophisticated global economy," said Dr. Lionel "Bo" Beaulieu, former director of the Southern Rural Development Center at Mississippi State University. For example, modern manufacturing plants began to use sophisticated technology and automation, which required higher levels of education and posteducation training. However, most schools made only slow improvements.

Through 2023, data showed many high schools doing a poor job preparing students for both work and higher education. The state continued to rank near the bottom in educational attainment. And business leaders began promoting career readiness assessments as more relevant than academic testing.

In 2020, the State Board of Education added the ACT WorkKeys assessment to its accountability system as part of its goal to prepare students for college and careers. The WorkKeys assessment measured foundational skills needed in the workplace. This came as communities across the state got their local schools to offer WorkKeys assessments so they could become ACT Work Ready Communities, a designation ACT said demonstrates they have aligned workforce development with economic development.

As used, WorkKeys assessed three areas—workplace documents (reading), applied math, and graphic literacy (locating information). WorkKeys National Career Readiness Certificates (NCRCs) were issued at four levels: bronze, silver, gold, and platinum. Simplified, the lower bronze level indicated readiness for entry-level jobs, silver readiness for blue and pink collar jobs, and gold readiness for white collar jobs. The platinum level indicated a rare combination of cognitive skills. Many industries came to recognize WorkKeys as a useful screening tool for new hires. A number began to require at least a silver level NCRC for employment. Lex Taylor, chairman of the Taylor Group of Companies, called the NCRC "essential to our hiring process."

How did Mississippi high school students do on the WorkKeys assessment?

Statewide results were not published by the MDE. However, The Montgomery Institute in Meridian worked with economic developers in Choctaw, Kemper, Webster, and Winston Counties from 2018 to 2021 to get WorkKeys assessments in their schools (all four counties became certified Work Ready Communities). Results showed that 696 high school seniors and a few juniors tested. Of these, 35.4 percent achieved the bronze level; 32 percent achieved the silver level; 11.7 percent achieved the gold level; and 5.8 percent achieved the platinum level (13.5 percent did not score well enough to receive a bronze-level

NCRC). The Mississippi page at the ACT Work Ready Communities website provided comparative date. It showed 174,571 NCRCs awarded in Mississippi from 2006 to 2022. This included adults, working and out of work, as well as students. Of these, 31.7 percent achieved bronze, 48.2 percent achieved silver, 15.7 percent achieved gold, and 4.4 percent achieved platinum (ACT did not publish the percentage that failed to achieve the bronze level).

What these data indicated was that 67 to 80 percent of students and adults were likely ready for entry-level and pink and blue collar jobs, but only 18 to 20 percent were likely ready for white collar and higher-level jobs. Unanswered was what to do with those who were unable to score at the bronze level besides remediation.

In 2022, CNBC reported, "At a time when companies are clamoring for skilled workers, Mississippi's workforce is among the nation's least educated, with the lowest concentration of STEM workers. It is also the least productive." It labeled Mississippi "the worst state for business."

In 2023, much more remained to get done to provide a good public education to all Mississippi children and prepare them for high-paying jobs.

HEALTH CARE

"For Lauderdale County, the lack of access to primary care for chronic, acute, and preventive care represents the major unmet health need for uninsured and underinsured residents, particularly African Americans. Not surprisingly, this underserved population has increasingly crowded into hospital emergency rooms believing this to be their only viable choice for care. In turn, the growing burden of uncompensated care is the major factor putting both of our two acute care hospitals in financial jeopardy."
—Community Health Improvement Network HRSA grant document

Health care was another pivotal issue that Mississippi's aginner sentiments led Republican legislators to dither over. I became intimately aware of Mississippi's challenges in this area through my work with the Community Health Improvement Network (CHIN) in Meridian, detailed research by Millsaps College intern Evan Jones, and the five years I served on the board of Anderson Regional Medical Center, a nonprofit hospital in Meridian.

Analysis conducted by CHIN revealed the gravity of the health care dilemmas facing Mississippi at the local level. When one of Meridian's two remaining acute care hospitals (in the 1980s there were five) announced in late 2015 that it was considering the closure of its emergency room due to excessive costs, The Montgomery Institute and the East Mississippi Development Corporation formed a broad-based community team to delve into the area's health care problems. A small planning grant was funded by the Health Resource and Services Administration of the US Department Health and Human Services to provide resources for the team to develop a strategic plan. CHIN was the result.

Data-driven research found emergency rooms in the community's two remaining acute care hospitals overcrowded, with uninsured and underinsured residents utilizing the ERs in place of primary care clinics, and levels of uncompensated care putting both hospitals at financial risk. Our research further identified significant gaps and barriers to health care services for a large portion of the county's population—29.52 percent of adults lacked a consistent source of primary care; 22.3 percent of adults aged eighteen to sixty-four (approximately 10,280 adults) were without health insurance; and 16 percent of the two hospitals' emergency room patients were uninsured.

Health care problems grew when the legislature decimated the Mississippi State Department of Health (MSDH) budget in 2013, causing it to reduce services at its local health clinics across the state. A March of Dimes report released in 2023 showed that fifty-one of the state's eighty-two counties were considered either maternity care deserts or having low access to maternity care. I wrote about the consequences.

MISSISSIPPI'S "MATERNITY CARE DESERTS" ABET MOM AND BABY DEATHS

August 6, 2023

"It's becoming ever more dangerous to give birth in America, especially for Black women, older women, and those living in rural areas, according to a pair of new reports from March of Dimes and the Milken Institute," reported Axios.

"Nationally, the maternal mortality rate in 2021 was 32.9 deaths per 100,000 live births—nearly double the 17.4 deaths per 100,000 live births in 2018, according to the CDC (Centers for Disease Control and Prevention)."

Mississippi, no surprise, had the highest rate among the states at 82.5 mom deaths per 100,000 live births.

Another no surprise, Mississippi still leads the nation in infant mortality.

"Mississippi led the nation with a rate of 10 deaths per 1,000 live births, almost twice the national rate of 5.73," reported Mississippi Today citing CDC data. Mississippi's number was 15 percent higher than the second-ranked state, Alabama.

A recent March of Dimes report labeled forty-two of Mississippi's eighty-two counties "maternity care deserts." These are counties with no OB-GYNs, certified nurse midwives, or hospitals that offer obstetric care. Another nine counties were deemed "low-access" areas.

Contributing to the problem are high rates of premature births and low birthweight babies, and low breastfeeding rates, categories in which Mississippi also rates the worst compared to other states.

The big picture nationally, said Axios, shows rural communities "struggling with health care access issues that go well beyond maternity care. And many obstetrics unit closures are about money, not politics."

That's Mississippi, too.

Financially strapped hospitals discontinuing maternity care and emergency rooms, depleted county health departments out of the clinical care business, and struggling rural counties unable to attract certified nurse midwives much less OB-GYNs largely describe the primary problem. Lack of health insurance, limited access to primary care, physician and nurse shortages, and limited transport options help describe larger access challenges.

State health officer Dr. Daniel Edney knows the problems but with limited resources can only take baby steps when giant steps are needed. Saving moms and babies requires increased access to obstetrics care—OB-GYNs, trained primary care physicians, certified nurse midwives, and birthing centers—in rural county after rural county across the state.

Good luck getting that.

The expansion of Medicaid postpartum insurance coverage earlier this year was a welcome but limited exception to the legislature's enduring legacy of indifference to maternal and infant mortality and declining health care access in rural areas.

In a different setting, that level of indifference would have been considered depraved indifference given its consequences—dead moms and babies who could have been saved.

"Don't fail to rescue those who are doomed to die." —Proverbs 24:11

March of Dimes also reported, "Women who delay or receive no prenatal care are more likely to deliver a low-birthweight infant or have a preterm birth compared to women receiving early care. Inadequate prenatal care is associated with an increased risk for neonatal death. Moreover, maternal mortality is significantly higher among rural populations." Mississippi already carried the label "worst state in the nation to give birth" since WLBT News published that headline in 2018. The label still applied in 2023.

Mississippi was also deemed the worst place to be old. The United Health Foundation in 2022 ranked Mississippi fiftieth in the nation for health care for seniors, just as it had since 2017. Among the categories analyzed, Mississippi ranked at the bottom for senior deaths, food insecurity, and isolation and in the bottom five for nursing home quality, avoiding care due to costs, physical inactivity, preventable hospitalizations, and poverty. I wrote about this.

MISSISSIPPI BACK ON BOTTOM IN SENIOR HEALTH RANKINGS

June 2, 2017

Mississippi is getting older. No, this is not about our bicentennial, but our people.

Since 1980, Mississippi's total population increased 18.5%, but the population of residents aged sixty-five and older jumped 43.3%. This pushed the median age up from 27.6 years in 1980 to 36.5 years in 2015. Over that time, the percentage of the population aged sixty-five and older moved from 11.5% to 14%.

Guess what, health rankings rate Mississippi the worst place to be old.

The United Health Foundation just released its latest America's Health Rankings: Senior Report. This is the fifth annual report. In the first two reports, Mississippi ranked fiftieth. We got off the bottom for two years. Now, we're back again, dead last in senior health.

The foundation says it publishes the senior health report to encourage "continued conversations among policymakers, public health officials, and community leaders" and to drive "action to promote better health for our nation's seniors."

The report's subtitle is "A Call to Action for Individuals and Their Communities." We'll have to see if Mississippi is paying attention.

The report does treat Mississippi kindly. It doesn't spotlight our bottom ranking. Rather, it says we're one of the three states "with the biggest opportunities for improvement." Nice twist. Kentucky (#49) and Oklahoma (#48) join us in these opportunities.

The rankings are based on thirty-four measures of senior health distributed among five categories. The categories and our ranking in each were: behaviors (45th), community and environment (50th), policy (41st), clinical care (47th), and outcomes (45th).

Interesting that our policies outrank our provisions for seniors.

The report included several lowlights and a few highlights for Mississippi.

Lowlights: In the past three years, food insecurity increased from 20.5% to 24.3% of adults aged sixty plus; in the past two years, volunteerism decreased from 25.3% to 20.3% of adults aged sixty-five plus; and since 2013, obesity increased from 27.9% to 30.8% of adults aged sixty-five plus.

Highlights: In the past three years, preventable hospitalizations decreased from 85.8 to 67.8 discharges per one thousand Medicare enrollees; in the past two years, poverty decreased from 14.3% to 12.5% of adults aged sixty-five plus;

and since 2013, the percentage of adults aged sixty-five plus with no disability increased from 54.0% to 57.4%.

We ranked in the bottom ten on seventeen of the thirty-four measures and in the top ten on only two.

The bottom-ten measures were: physical inactivity, obesity, dental care, poverty, volunteerism, community support, food insecurity, number of geriatricians, health screenings, hip fractures, hospital deaths, hospital readmissions, preventable hospitalizations, percentage able-bodied, self-reported high health status, premature deaths, and tooth extractions.

The top-ten measures were: excessive drinking, with only an estimated 3.9% of seniors indulging at that level; and pain management, with 50.6% of seniors with arthritis who reported that related pain does not limit their usual activities.

Oh, the top five states for senior health were Minnesota, Utah, Hawaii, Colorado, and New Hampshire. The top-ranked state in the cluster around Mississippi was Alabama at forty-third.

The state and national turmoil surrounding health care funding suggests our ranking is unlikely to improve any time soon.

Stay healthy, my fellow seniors.

The folks in between birth and old age also dwelt in a low-rated health care environment. In 2022, the Commonwealth Fund ranked Mississippi last in the nation for health system performance. Factors securing the state's bottom ranking included low ratings for access and affordability, prevention and treatment, avoidable hospital use and cost, and racial and ethnic equity. *U.S. News and World Report* ranked Mississippi next to last in overall health care based on health care quality (fiftieth), public health (forty-sixth), and health care access (forty-fifth). Fox Business News reported on a WalletHub report ranking Mississippi's health care system at the bottom, based on forty-two factors grouped into three broad categories—cost, access, and outcomes. HealthCare-Insider ranked Mississippi last for mental health care based on three factors—cost, access, and quality.

Confounding the problems were shortages of doctors and nurses. In 2022, all but four of Mississippi's eighty-two counties were designated Primary Care Health Professional Shortage Areas; parts of the other four counties were similarly rated. The Mississippi Hospital Association reported state hospitals short 3,038 registered nurses in 2022. One in four RN positions were vacant, with numbers much higher in rural areas.

Most problematic, however, was the growing plight of hospitals. Between 2013 and 2022, five rural hospitals had closed and roughly half of those remaining were struggling financially. In 2023, the legislature, instead of expanding Medicaid, appropriated $103 million to contribute to hospitals based on number of beds. One hospital estimated this would help pay for just one month of operations. Fortunately, Mississippi Medicaid also increased some reimbursements. Yet, at-risk hospitals continued to shed services. Labor and delivery services were among the first to go—from Hancock Medical Center in Bay St. Louis to Delta Regional Medical Center in Greenville. Dr. Daniel P. Edney, the state health officer, warned this could result in "health care deserts."

Some hospitals showed interest in shedding inpatient care to survive. The new federal "rural emergency hospital" program would provide annual "facility payments" estimated at $3.2 million for hospitals to abandon inpatient care and operate simply as emergency rooms. While this might keep emergency care available, those rural hospitals' days as major local employers and community economic engines would end.

Governor Tate Reeves, House Speaker Philip Gunn, and their Republican minions obstructed opportunities to expand Medicaid. Cost was their first argument. When that proved no longer to be a real issue, their real reason was exposed—political ideology. "I am opposed to Obamacare expansion," Reeves said over and over. "I've always maintained, to the extent that we can, decreased government dependency, that should be the goal," Gunn said on SuperTalk Radio. "Expansion in my view is going in the opposite direction."

Greenwood Commonwealth publisher Tim Kalich called their positions "hard-headed and hard-hearted," as he watched his local hospital, Greenwood Leflore Hospital, shed services and head toward closure.

Governor Reeves's position got challenged by former University of Mississippi chancellor Dr. Dan Jones. I wrote about that.

GOVERNOR SLAMS RESPECTED FORMER CHANCELLOR

February 12, 2023

"I'd bet I hadn't talked to this dude since well before he was fired by Ole Miss," tweeted Gov. Tate Reeves.

"This dude!" Really?

The "dude" referred to was Dr. Dan Jones, the highly respected and much beloved former chancellor of the University of Mississippi, the university's former distinguished vice chancellor for health affairs and dean of the medical school, the accomplished physician and former medical missionary to Korea, and the recently retired director of the Mississippi Center for Obesity Research.

Also, Dan was never fired by Ole Miss. The IHL board chose not to renew his contract as chancellor in 2015 when he unwaveringly stood behind his successors at the medical center in the face of strong board intrusion into its operations.

The governor issued his caustic tweet after Dan revealed a conversation he had with Reeves during his time as chancellor.

"A little while after I began explaining the benefits of Medicaid expansion, he [Reeves] put his hand up and said, 'Chancellor, I recognize it would be good for Mississippians, good for our economy, good for health care if we expanded Medicaid,'" Dan recalled in a recent press conference. "I had a big smile on my face and said, 'I'm so glad to hear you're going to support expansion.' His response: 'Oh no, I'm not going to support it because it's not in my personal political interest.'"

Reeves's tweet called Jones's comments an "obvious lie," adding, "I never would have said this."

Unfortunately, the governor may well have said something like that. He has had similar conversations in private about PERS' financial woes.

A self-proclaimed numbers guy, former state treasurer, former lieutenant governor, and now governor, Reeves understands more than most the financial plight of hospitals, the true costs and benefits of Medicaid expansion, and the never-ending funding dilemmas at PERS.

While lieutenant governor, he once said, "The fact our pension funding levels are weak and getting weaker, that's a real issue. But heretofore, there has not been the political will to do anything about it."

An early supporter, I began to doubt Tate's competence to lead when he as lieutenant governor ducked the PERS issue after Gov. Haley Barbour's PERS study commission issued its detailed report. He confirmed that doubt when he ignored the plight of hospitals.

The sad truth is that none have lacked the political will to tackle PERS and health care issues more than Tate Reeves. He has feared, as Dan Jones recounted, potential negative impacts on his political ambitions.

Had Dan been more of a political creature like the governor, enraptured with his own ambitions, he would still be chancellor at Ole Miss. Kudos to the "dude" for speaking out.

"Do nothing out of selfish ambition or vain conceit." —Philippians 2:3

Few actions would have helped pry Mississippi off the bottom in more areas more quickly than expanding Medicaid. Providing access to affordable health care to the working poor would have begun to reduce deaths from lack of care for obesity, heart disease, stroke, septicemia, and cancer. Expansion would have created thousands of new jobs, helped reduce single-parent households, improved per capita income, and upped workforce participation. It would also have provided a needed financial lifeline to rural hospitals.

RURAL MISSISSIPPI

In the early 1990s, the Ford Foundation assessed dilemmas impacting rural places. Finding many "tough challenges," the foundation reported: "Creating quality jobs, giving kids a shot at a good education, providing decent health care, providing opportunities for more people to take an active role in shaping the future of their communities, and creating hope for the future represent just a handful of the key issues facing many rural communities today."

Mississippi is a rural state. Failure to adopt policies and plans to strengthen rural areas provided another example of political insanity.

Numerous trends in rural counties and towns pointed to problems. I wrote about those trends.

STUDY SHOWS RURAL MISSISSIPPI DRIFTING INTO DISTRESS

May 27, 2019

"What was once a country of disparate places that converged toward prosperity is now a country of places drifting further apart," reports the bipartisan Economic Innovation Group (EIG). Rural areas are the most impacted.

The EIG study found population increasing in the better-off counties while it was declining in the worse-off counties. Population, however, was not used as a measure. The study used these criteria: (1) percentage of the adult population with no high school diploma, (2) housing vacancy rate, (3) percentage of working-age adults not working, (4) poverty rate, (5) ratio of county income over state income, (6) change in number of jobs, and (7) change in number of businesses.

From these criteria, the EIG performed a county-by-county comparison using two distinct time periods, 2007–2011 and 2012–2016.

What the study showed was a "great reshuffling" following the Great Recession.

"In the years following the recession, top-tier places have thrived, seeing meteoric growth in jobs, businesses, and population. Meanwhile, the number of people living in America's most distressed zip codes is shrinking as the nature of distress becomes more rural."

The study further notes that the gaps in well-being between prosperous areas and other areas have grown wider.

Mississippi had nine counties rated better off in both periods analyzed while seventy-three were rated worse off. DeSoto, Madison, Rankin, Lafayette, Lamar, Lee, and Jackson were rated better off in both periods. Marshall and Tate replaced Harrison and George in the later period.

The study showed only 7% of Mississippians residing in prosperous zip codes (second only to West Virginia), while 41.9% resided in distressed zip codes (the highest proportion among all states).

Other findings included: (1) prosperous zip codes were home to lots of professional workers while at-risk zip codes were home to lots of blue collar workers;

(2) minorities were overrepresented in distressed communities; (3) prosperous communities added more net new businesses than the other 80% percent of zip codes combined from 2012 to 2016; (4) Americans in marginal communities continued to fall out of work deep into the recovery; and (5) the geography of well-being largely reflects the geography of college-educated workers.

Looking at changes since the Great Recession, the EIG reported, "Amid the reshuffling wrought by the fractured recovery, educational attainment has emerged as the sharpest fault-line separating thriving communities from struggling ones. Urban areas are ascendant, rural areas are in flux, and suburbs retain their outsize claim on the map of US prosperity."

(Another study projected that by 2040 over 85% of the US population will live in urban areas.)

The EIG study concluded with this message: "Positive national statistics must not blind us to these divergent local realities or breed complacency in our needed efforts to expand access to opportunity to new corners of the country."

The same goes for Mississippi. Positive statewide statistics driven by a handful of counties must not blind us to distressing realities in our rural counties.

Note to conservatives: the EIG sees capitalism as the means to revitalize worse-off counties in three ways: (1) private investment, (2) entrepreneurship and the growth of new business (3) a more innovative and accessible US economy.

Data analysis in 2021 for most rural counties in Mississippi showed per capita income and educational attainment levels below the state's low averages, population decreasing with the proportion of elderly people increasing, bright people migrating to urban areas with better job and lifestyle opportunities, plus significant teacher, nurse, and physician shortages. As noted earlier, forty-three of Mississippi's eighty-two counties, mostly rural, suffered from persistent poverty. Such data caused David Rumbarger, president and CEO of the Community Development Foundation in Lee County, to tell the *Northeast Mississippi Daily Journal*: "Smaller, rural communities are still struggling to maintain and grow." Other challenges continued to mount.

Rural legislators, if they understood the data, made no demands for the state to take action. Truth managers pushing income tax cuts appeared to have more influence over rural legislators than trend data. I wrote about that.

FIREFIGHTER SHORTAGE HIGHLIGHTS, AGAIN, NEED FOR RURAL PLAN

August 7, 2022

Mississippi remains mostly rural. Rural areas continue to struggle. New issues continue to arise. Still, the state appears to have no comprehensive plan to aid rural areas.

You can add a growing shortage of volunteer firefighters to the known list of rural issues. Last week, the *Northeast Mississippi Daily Journal* documented problems facing Lee County.

"There are several departments throughout the county that are just not getting the response because they don't have enough volunteers," District 1 supervisor Phil Morgan told the *Journal*. "My concern is the fact that we're getting to the numbers where it's not safe anymore for the firefighters," Marc Flanagan, Lee County's fire coordinator, said. "If there's a chance of a rescue, someone has got to go in, and you can't make entry with two people on the scene."

Not long ago, WCBI News in Columbus reported a major shortage of volunteer firefighters in rural Lowndes County.

The National Fire Protection Association has raised concerns about the declining number of firefighters. Declining fire response capabilities carry a double whammy. In addition to fire disasters, home insurance rates can surge. As reported by the Journal, "fire ratings influence insurance rates, and fire ratings are based on many factors, including the number of firefighters that are locally available, the number and type of trucks, whether fire hydrants are available, and so on."

Remember the other items already on the list?

Population changes. Rural areas are losing population, and the remaining population is aging. Just in the seventeen counties served by the CREATE Foundation in northeast Mississippi, "twelve of our seventeen counties are losing population," reported Lewis Whitfield, senior vice president of the foundation.

Brain drain. State Auditor Shad White calls that one of the state's most challenging issues.

Nursing shortages. Hospitals have reported increasing vacancy rates and difficulty recruiting experienced nurses. Some rural nursing homes, clinics, and hospitals have reported turnover rates from 36% to 50%.

Teacher shortages. This year's pay raises may help, but the State Department of Education reported that nearly one of every three school districts in Mississippi is designated a critical teacher shortage area. The solution will take more than this pay increase.

Rural infrastructure. Crumbling roads and bridges plus antique water and sewage facilities may get some relief from recent federal infrastructure grants, but many problems will remain.

Health care. Too many uninsured persons, lack of physicians, and struggling hospitals contribute to high infant mortality, obesity, and other mortality rates. Also, the national Centers for Disease Control reported that people in rural areas were four times more likely to die from drug overdoses now than a decade ago. And the age-adjusted suicide rate for the most rural counties was 1.8 times the rate for urban counties.

Economic distress. Rural areas are major contributors to Mississippi's bad rankings on poverty, wage rates, workforce participation rates, educational achievement, and more.

Lack of a coordinated, long-term plan to address these issues portends a bleak future for more rural Mississippians.

"Rescue the weak and needy." —Psalm 82:4

It wasn't as if state leaders had never heard of how a plan could benefit rural areas. For example, in late 2005 Mississippi governor Haley Barbour and Alabama governor Bob Riley helped The Montgomery Institute land a $15 million, four-year Workforce Innovation in Regional Economic Development (WIRED) grant from the US Department of Labor. Key partners were four community colleges in east Mississippi and four in west Alabama, all serving thirty-seven rural counties with 158 communities. With expert support from the national Rural Policy Research Institute (RUPRI), Mississippi State University, the University of Alabama, the Center for Adult and Experiential Learning, and the Auburn University Urban Studio, leaders from those communities developed a comprehensive strategic plan with three major goals: (1) help rural communities identify assets and strengths and initiate place-building efforts to retain/attract jobs and residents; (2) help rural communities develop support systems and policies to encourage local entrepreneurship and set up an online system to support and train entrepreneurs; and (3) develop a regional training framework utilizing new equipment and training tools to build a more competitive workforce, add nationally recognized credentials to training programs beginning with the WorkKeys Career Readiness certification, and set up an online advanced manufacturing training system.

Numerous other initiatives, including those promoted by the Appalachian Regional Commission and the Delta Regional Authority (I represented Governor Barbour on both during my time at the Mississippi Development Authority [MDA]), showed means and methods to help rural Mississippi. However, state leadership never adopted a statewide plan to deal with rural economic distress.

POVERTY

Poor quality of life produces children very unready for learning, which weakens schools, which weakens the workforce, which weakens the economy, which weakens the quality of life. Around and around it goes, spiraling downward toward poverty. This is how the Iron Circle of Poverty functions.

Indifference resulting from our behavioral shadows has kept Mississippi from breaking its Iron Circle of Poverty.

In the summer of 2019, the Phil Hardin Foundation in Meridian brought ten Millsaps College students into the community to work as interns with various agencies. Assignments varied, but political science major Evan Jones got to do some interesting research. His task was to investigate key social and economic challenges facing the city. After documenting population trends and increasing disparities in income, educational achievement, and racial composition, Jones came across data he found shocking—the plight of single mothers, particularly those of color, and their children. He found that poverty, low educational achievement, and little access to health care were common characteristics. He found the proportion of single-mother households in Meridian surprisingly high and persistent. He researched this information after noticing the high rates of teen pregnancy and high incidence of low birth-weight babies in the city. He called these trends "a catalyst for the cycle of poverty." I wrote about this.

LEGISLATIVE GROUPS SHOULD TARGET DECLINING COMMUNITIES, DISCONNECTED YOUTH

July 26, 2016

As legislators gather in their working groups to study programs and budgets, they should also take note of long-term phenomena with significant impacts.

One of these is a downward spiral that can cripple communities. It's named the "Iron Circle of Poverty." It's called the "iron circle" because it is extremely hard to break. Few communities have the talented leadership and sense of common purpose needed to do so. Without help from state leadership and resources, many will not.

Big events or a number of small, sustained events can trigger the downward spiral. Loss of major employers and natural disasters are big events that can kick off the spiral. Population declines, loss of locally owned businesses, lack of new capital investment, aging housing stock, escalating property taxes, an aging and unskilled workforce, middle- to upper-class residential flight (usually white), growing criminal activity, and declining schools are examples of trends that can aggregate over time and launch the spiral.

Once started, the downward spiral gains momentum as interconnected facets of the community weaken each other, for instance the local economy slows, quality of life begins to decline, housing stock and infrastructure age without repair, schools deteriorate and qualified teachers leave, the workforce degrades, capital investment slows, job openings dry up, the economy slows further. . . . Around and around it goes, spiraling downward. Along the way, poverty and crime surge.

What are the state's plan, its policies, and its resources that communities caught in the iron circle can access? Oh, there are pieces and parts, but no comprehensive help for downward-spiraling communities. Some legislative working group should look into this.

Another long-term phenomenon of great impact is the escalation of violence and gang activity among at-risk youth. Too many are becoming disconnected from traditional pathways that lead to success as adults. They become easy prey for gangs and fall into behaviors that leave them even more disconnected. Community leaders tend to look to the juvenile part of our criminal justice system to rectify the problem. But often, the problem is too widespread and deep rooted for the juvenile system to handle, much less resolve.

Research shows that communities wanting to interrupt gang recruitment and cycles of violence for youth must institute a range of complementary programs. Early childhood education is one key component, but not the end-all. After-school programs, summer youth programs, youth employment programs, and safe places and counseling for abused children are examples of other programs that together with early childhood education can have impact. But, the programs must reach most at-risk children, not just a small percentage, and must be sustained over time.

State leaders tend to look at early childhood education, juvenile justice, mental health, law enforcement, and youth programs as stand-alone programs. They need to be considered as complementary components of a vital system if we are to effectively deal with our growing disconnected youth problem.

Budgets and taxes are important topics for working groups, but so too are long-term phenomena that destroy communities and youth.

In contrast to the Iron Circle of Poverty, research shows that states, regions, and communities will spiral upward in prosperity through consistent and persevering efforts to provide good schools, a skilled workforce, a strong economy, and a high quality of life. In 2001 as the president of The Montgomery Institute, I worked with the Phil Hardin Foundation on a rigorous thinking project to develop "key benchmarks" to provide both data and measures leaders could use to track upward progress.

Twenty-four benchmarks were developed with help from State Superintendent of Education Dr. Henry Johnson, Southern Rural Development Center director Dr. Lionel "Bo" Beaulieu, University of Mississippi Advanced Education Center director Dr. Charles Harrison, Education Research Center Bureau of Long-Range Economic Planning director Pete Walley, and Mississippi State University associate professor of educational leadership Dr. Elizabeth Burns.

Cycle of Prosperity Benchmarks for Accountability and Decision Making

1. Children will be ready to enter kindergarten.
2. Third-grade students will be proficient in reading.
3. Seventh-grade students will be proficient in math.
4. ACT scores will reach the Southeastern average.
5. Teachers will be highly qualified.
6. Schools will be highly rated.
7. Schools will be safe.
8. Students will graduate from high school.
9. Workers without diplomas will obtain GEDs.
10. Nontraditional students will enroll in college.
11. Students will complete college.
12. Higher education levels will be attained.
13. Workers will become skilled workers.
14. Workers will be employed in productive jobs.
15. Workers will earn high wages.
16. Businesses will do well.
17. Areas will grow their economies.
18. Incomes will approach the US average.
19. Minority income will achieve parity.
20. Public safety will be preserved.
21. Home ownership will increase.
22. Citizens will be healthy.
23. Families will be stronger.
24. Conditions for children will improve.

Each benchmark required one or more data sets to be tracked. For example, the "families will be stronger" benchmark would be measured by trends in divorces, teen pregnancy rates, numbers of children in two-parent families, and numbers of births to unwed mothers. Consistent progress on these benchmarks would move a community upward into a Cycle of Prosperity. Consistent progress across the state would begin to move Mississippi off the bottom.

Upon joining Haley Barbour's team at the MDA in 2004, I altered the twenty-four benchmarks into two more easily managed indexes to conform with his Momentum Mississippi agenda. One that we called the Boom Index, adapted from Jack Schultz's indicators of prosperity in *Boom Town USA: The 7½ Keys to Big Success in Small Towns*, would simply measure annual gains or losses on three indicators for which timely data could be obtained. Schultz contended that annual progress on all three would signify boom status for a community. The three indicators were:

population growth,
job growth, and
wage growth.

The second index, which we called the Momentum Index—drawn from our twenty-four benchmarks but easier to measure—would track ten indicators. Improving trends on these would indicate momentum toward prosperity. The ten indicators were:

home ownership,
crime rates,
births to unwed mothers,
high school graduation rates,
third-grade reading proficiency,
cardiovascular disease rates,
obesity rates,
population growth rates,
workforce participation rates, and
per capita income.

Unfortunately, both of these efforts to rigorously track and utilize data to spur local and state development activities fell mostly on deaf ears, even though many of the benchmarks and indicators rated as highly with site selection firms as tax rates. I wrote about our prosperity indicators.

PROSPERITY INDICATORS NOT SO GOOD ACROSS MISSISSIPPI

April 29, 2019

Mississippi politicians running for reelection or higher office are out, about, and on social media touting how good things are and how they helped make things that way.

Well, some things are good, but some are far from good. One is population growth, or rather, lack thereof.

As Jack Schultz noted in his best seller *Boomtown USA*, population growth is one of the best indicators of an area's prosperity. People, especially young people, gravitate to booming economies with good quality of life.

So, when you talk to your favorite politicians, ask them to explain why all those good things happening in Mississippi are not resulting in population growth.

Here's some background.

The Census Bureau recently released data on county population changes. Based on this, Business Insider published the top ten fastest-growing counties in America and the top ten fastest-shrinking counties in America. Guess which list included Mississippi counties?

Texas, Florida, North Carolina, and North Dakota had all the fastest-growing counties.

Mississippi had two of the fastest-shrinking counties, Washington and Coahoma. Louisiana also had two. Other states on the list were Alabama, Arkansas, Florida, Kansas, Louisiana, and Missouri.

In fact, most Mississippi counties are shrinking in population.

From 2010 to 2018, Census Bureau data showed that sixty-three of Mississippi's eighty-two counties lost population. Fourteen showed measurable growth, while five showed no change.

Nine counties showed double-digit percentage population losses—Washington, Leflore, Coahoma, Sunflower, Jefferson Davis, Quitman, Humphreys, Wilkinson, and Sharkey, all Delta counties except Jefferson Davis and Wilkinson.

Five counties showed double-digit growth—Lafayette, DeSoto, Madison, Lamar, and Harrison, all urban except Lafayette (home to the University of Mississippi).

Of note, seven of our seventeen urban (metropolitan area) counties showed growth, but only seven of our sixty-five rural counties showed growth. Uh, most of our politicians represent rural areas.

Then there's this.

"Counties Where the American Dream Is Dead," headlines a story in USA Today that lists fifty such counties, thirteen of them in Mississippi: Coahoma, Humphreys, Tunica, Claiborne, Leflore, Hinds, Tallahatchie, Sunflower, Bolivar, Oktibbeha, Washington, Grenada, and Quitman. (All lost population except Oktibbeha, home to Mississippi State University.)

The story says the opportunity to achieve the American dream is virtually dead for young people living in these counties.

The results come from a 24/7 Wall St. review of data published by the Equality of Opportunity Project, tax returns from 1996 to 2012, and US Census data.

The Equality of Opportunity Project, part of a Harvard University program, looked at the likelihood of twenty-six-year-olds achieving upward income mobility on a county-by-county basis. The project researchers found little hope and low probability for young people raised in low-income counties to earn more as adults than the average annual income for the bottom quartile of earners nationally. Every year spent in such counties decreased their opportunities for success.

Declining population, particularly in rural counties, and declining hopes for many young people are not good things or indicators of prosperity.

You probably won't hear much about this from politicians running for reelection or higher office.

During the period from 1975 to early 2023 covered by this narrative, Mississippi remained at or near the bottom in national rankings. That is not to say the state did not make any progress. It did. For example, average annual pay in private industry more than doubled to $44,353 in 2021 but remained at the bottom and $5,000 below the next-lowest state, West Virginia. The poverty rate improved from 23.9 percent in 1980 to 19 percent in 2022 but remained worst in the nation. However, neither Democrats while they were in charge nor Republicans since they took over could pry Mississippi off the bottom.

In my experience from attempts to utilize the Cycle of Prosperity benchmarks, Mississippi, with a few notable exceptions, lacked a culture of rigorous thinking that valued using research and data analysis to inform decisions. Sometimes, Mississippians seemed indifferent to data, particularly when it related to poverty and related issues. At least that attitude was often reflected as Republican power surged to control of the governor's office and the legislature. For example, so-called efforts to eliminate waste and fraud in various federally funded and subsidized poverty programs resulted in onerous paperwork, bureaucratic delays, and failure to fully expend funds despite high demand.

Nothing exposed this trend more than the misuse of Temporary Assistance for Needy Families (TANF) funds. The Associated Press reported a dramatic decrease in TANF funds actually going to needy families soon after Governor Phil Bryant took office. Millions of dollars were simply not spent. Later, State Auditor Shad White discovered that other millions of TANF dollars were inappropriately and illegally spent. The purpose of TANF, which replaced the Aid to Families with Dependent Children welfare program during the Clinton administration, was to provide income support for poor families, promote self-sufficiency including employment, encourage two-parent families, and reduce out-of-wedlock births. Properly coordinated with other programs, TANF resources could make a difference for many of the left out and left behind.

I wrote about Mississippi's "strategy" to eradicate poverty.

HOLE IN THE WHOLE THWARTS POVERTY ERADICATION

August 29, 2022

Congress has begun paying more attention to counties whose poverty rates persist at 20% or more over a thirty-year period. Forty-three of Mississippi's eighty-two counties rate among these "persistent poverty counties," according to the Congressional Research Service.

The 2022 report said that up to 15.9% of the nation's 3,143 counties suffer persistent poverty. But Mississippi's ratio was triple that, at 52.4%.

What is Mississippi's strategy to address persistent poverty in these counties?

Well, there is a statewide goal, often expressed as "moving people from poverty to prosperity." Of course, a glib goal is neither a strategy nor a plan.

The concept that Mississippi leaders appear to have embraced is that putting people to work will eradicate poverty. So, the state has invested heavily in basic skills and workforce training to prepare poor people with few skills for jobs.

The State Workforce Investment Board, called the SWIB, controls state and federal dollars to fund these programs. Federal dollars go into programs for "out-of-school youth" and adult "dislocated workers" coordinated through regional Workforce Investment Boards and planning and development districts. State dollars mostly go into community college training programs but also into targeted training programs run by other organizations.

However, training programs are not available in all areas, so daily transportation is a problem for many. Lack of money to pay fees is another.

The federally funded Temporary Assistance for Needy Families (TANF) program, managed by the Mississippi Department of Human Services, also has a role in placing poor people into jobs.

However, we have seen TANF money corruptly siphoned off and used for other purposes. And in many years, the state somehow has been unable to use all its TANF funds despite thousands of unaccepted applications.

Despite all the training that is available, the lack of available jobs in rural, persistently poor counties makes it tough to put people to work in their home areas.

Then there is the hole in the whole—the great big hole in the whole scheme. In Mississippi, putting people to work often does not alleviate poverty. With the lowest average wages in the nation, Mississippi has many hardworking people who earn so little they remain in poverty.

Indeed, many poor people find themselves worse off when they take low-wage jobs. Costs for child care and traveling eat up limited income. Rent subsidies and charitable care in emergency rooms disappear. When they get behind on bills, their meager pay can be garnished.

Tough, say the politicians who determine state policies. Taxpayers shouldn't bear their burdens. Cut back on federally funded subsidies, tighten up access, and make 'em go to work.

Alternatively, places committed to working with poor families have plugged the hole. Using well-coordinated federal, state, and local resources sustained over time, they step many families out of poverty.

In Mississippi, the mechanisms are in place, but not sustained commitment and coordination. Instead, we sustain our persistent poverty, low wages, world-leading incarceration rate, and nation-lowest workforce participation rate.

"But because of your hard and impenitent heart you are storing up wrath for yourself." —Romans 2:5.

In 2015, the *Guardian* wrote a lengthy article about Tchula, Mississippi, which it identified as among the four lowest-income towns in the country. "The people are sick, the people are uneducated, the people are poor because of an economic system that goes back to slavery," said Dr. Ronald Myers, who established a clinic for low-income families in Tchula in 1988.

So, what has been Republican leaders' approach to poverty when it is the root of so many of Mississippi's bottom-hugging dilemmas? Indifference.

SUMMARY

The legislature's unwillingness to provide the means for a good education to all children and its failure to provide for early interventions for at-risk children have undermined state efforts to improve educational achievement and build a highly competitive workforce. Expecting different results while continually underfunding education is another example of political insanity.

Republican leaders' failure to deal with the state's dire health care issues left mothers and babies at risk, put the state's hospitals at risk of closure, and undermined public health. It was another huge hole in the whole and another manifestation of Faulkner's curse, the double whammy, and political insanity.

As evidence mounted that more and more rural Mississippi counties were drifting toward distress, the state's Republican leadership failed to react. Ignoring problems and expecting things to improve was another form of insanity.

State leaders had no plan to alleviate poverty in poverty-ridden Mississippi. Cycle of Prosperity benchmarks identified policy areas that if addressed would begin to lift Mississippi off the bottom. Misuse of poverty funds illustrated Republican leaders' indifference to Mississippi's greatest dilemma.

A few improvements have been made in recent years, but these results illustrate Mississippi's need for good government conservatives in leadership roles.

Chapter Five

HOW TO SOLVE MISSISSIPPI'S COMPLEX DILEMMAS

RIGOROUS THINKING

Herein lies the motivation behind my approach to column writing. I use facts and data to challenge propaganda and propagandists in order to incite people to think for themselves . . . not just willy-nilly thinking, but rigorous thinking. Educators today call it critical thinking.

I once told the annual meeting of the Union County Development Association that Mississippi simply needed to follow the approach used by a famous English philosopher and strategist. When faced with a daunting dilemma, Winnie-the-Pooh would put a paw to his head, concentrate, and mutter "think, think" to discover a solution. If a bear of very little brain like Winnie-the-Pooh used thinking to solve tough problems, perhaps Mississippians could, too.

The dilemmas holding Mississippi to the bottom are intractable but not unsolvable. Solutions abound. Our failures to provide those solutions for our dilemmas further expose our holes in the whole. Henry Ford said, "Failure is simply opportunity to begin again, this time more intelligently." We Mississippians have begun again and again to solve our dilemmas yet have struggled to employ the "more intelligently" piece. Rigorous, strategic thinking is the first step needed to begin closing holes. I wrote about this.

FLOOD SPOTLIGHTS NEED FOR STRATEGIC POLICY THINKING

February 21, 2020

Politicians tend to be adept at tactical political thinking. How do I win the next election? How do I get this project my financial backers want approved? How do I keep special interest groups on my side? And so on.

Strategic policy thinking to solve systemic and long-term problems, well, that's another story.

Effective government, however, cannot be singularly driven by tactical political thinking. Strategic policy thinking has a critical role.

As state and local officials assess the decimating impact of the 2020 Pearl River flood, flood control is an appropriate example of the need for strategic policy thinking.

Flood control and prevention seldom occupy public officials' minds . . . until a flood happens. Of course, then, all the tactical political thinking in the world is too late to help the victims.

Flood control and prevention require rigorous, strategic thinking over time, and difficult, often costly decisions at the federal, state, and local levels.

Our more elderly leaders will remember the construction of Sardis, Arkabutla, Enid, and Grenada Lakes as flood control projects. These were made possible by the federal Flood Control Act of 1937, a reaction to the Great Mississippi Flood of 1927. The multimillion dollar project took two decades to complete, starting with Sardis in the 1930s, followed by Arkabutla and Enid, and concluding with Grenada in 1954. Hard decisions included completely relocating the town of Coldwater.

Following the great Easter flood on the Pearl River in 1979, numerous flood control and prevention ideas were proposed. But, as WLBT News reported in 2016, none were implemented. The latest is the $355 million One Lake project, which, while primarily an economic development project, would also provide flood control benefits.

(Many think the Ross Barnett Reservoir is a flood control lake. But it was built in the 1960s primarily as a water supply source with potential economic development as a major factor.)

Until this month, Pearl River flooding occupied few leaders' minds. Now, for a while, it will. The One Lake project appears to have been rigorously planned, but will federal, state, and local leaders agree on the difficult and costly decisions needed to build it? Is it comprehensive enough?

You would hope so. But other strategic policy solutions based on rigorous study have fizzled due to tactical political thinking. The most prominent, of course, is the Mississippi Economic Council's 2015 study of roads and bridges. The study documented maintenance needs and proposed solutions. The conservative Tax Foundation concurred in the method to fund needed repairs. Efforts to raise fuel taxes fell prey to tactical political thinking that taxpayers would unelect Republican leaders.

Then there are systemic problems that most politicians don't seriously study, much less resolve. Aging water and sewer systems, aging public school facilities, and a stressed trauma care system are examples.

You would think that a state that ranks fiftieth in so many areas would make strategic policy thinking a top priority. Regrettably, politicians these days seldom turn to studies or rely on objective experts to craft solutions. The consequence is ineffective government and worsening systemic problems. The only ray of hope I see is Lt. Gov. Delbert Hosemann. He gets it.

"Make plans by seeking advice." —Proverbs 20:18

The hospital crisis provided another example of state leaders' failure to utilize rigorous strategic thinking to plan for the future. I wrote about this, too.

HOSPITAL CLOSURES NOW, UNIVERSITIES NEXT?

November 27, 2022

"What's your plan: to watch Rome burn and to let hospitals close?" a Louisiana health care expert asked regarding Mississippi's hospital crisis.

Think about that. State leaders have sat on their hands and watched the state's hospital crisis build for more than a decade. As the *Northeast Mississippi Daily Journal* wrote recently, "Nothing has had a larger impact than the loss of federal dollars hospitals use to offset losses from care provided to uninsured patients.

That money started shrinking more than a decade ago with the passage of the Affordable Care Act. It was to be offset by expanding Medicaid coverage to the working poor."

Mississippi leaders didn't. And they came up with no alternative plan.

Our leaders seem to have trouble looking ahead, much less effectively planning ahead. For over two decades they have watched PERS finances deteriorate and prison problems mount. More recently, brain drain and rural population loss trends seemed to catch them by surprise.

Now comes another potential crisis. "The population of college-age Americans is about to crash," reports an article at Vox. "It will change higher education forever."

The problem arises from declining birthrates in America. "The birthrate kept dropping, and we are now starting to see the consequences on campuses everywhere," said the Vox article. "Classes will shrink, year after year, for most of the next two decades. People in the higher education industry call it 'the enrollment cliff.'"

Mississippi is not exempt from this demographic trend. Live births have declined by over 18% since 2000. In-state resident enrollment in our universities has now begun to drop. From 2013 to 2021, IHL in-state enrollment fell 14%. While that was partially offset by out-of-state student increases, overall enrollment is trending down. Note, out-of-state enrollment now accounts for one-third of IHL enrollment.

Mississippi Valley State University announced this month that its enrollment had fallen 9% to its lowest level in decades. "The current enrollment challenges are happening nationally, and as the numbers showed for our eight public institutions here in Mississippi, seven experienced an enrollment decline this fall," MVSU president Jerryl Briggs told the Greenwood Commonwealth. IHL system enrollment was down 1% this year. It has fallen each year since 2016 for a cumulative decline of 8%.

Notably, from 2016 to 2021 IHL freshman enrollment dropped 23%.

Already having to regularly increase tuition and fees due to declining state support, IHL universities will have trouble dealing with long-term enrollment decreases. While not a crisis yet, except at the Valley, it could become one if the trends of enrollment drops and state support continue. Declining birthrates predict that the enrollment trend will.

So, what is the state's forward-looking plan to deal with this? Without one, my old favorite issue will likely raise its head—closing and merging institutions. Since the "let 'em burn" approach is in vogue for hospitals, universities need to get ready.

"So, if you think you are standing firm, be careful that you don't fall." —1 Corinthians 10:12

Writing for newspapers taught me to think rigorously about facts. A diploma in financial management and control from the School for Bank Administration at the University of Wisconsin and numerous Sheshunoff financial seminars taught me how to apply rigorous thinking. When my bank hit troubled times and promoted me to executive vice president and chief financial officer, I used those skills to guide the bank back to profitability. I also found an error in the complex formula the Federal Reserve Bank of Atlanta, New Orleans Branch, used to calculate the bank's reserve requirement. Finding that error led to a multimillion dollar reserve credit at a time of exorbitant interest rates, a tremendous boon to the bank. Rigorous thinking also got me labeled as the financial "architect" of the College Board's *Ayers* settlement in 1999. Knowing that the legislature would balk at a huge lump sum payout, I devised a multiyear, phased financial strategy to fund the settlement plan. The total would be significant, but the annual impact would be reasonable.

In 2012, Meridian mayor Cheri Barry asked me to chair the Meridian Urban Renewal Authority. Our major task was to work with a developer to secure new market tax credits to fund a new city law enforcement center. My rigorous review of the developers' proposed plan led to adjustments in the cash flow projections to make certain that funds passed through the developer came back to the authority to retire the loans.

After I founded The Montgomery Institute in 2001, grant writing became a major responsibility in our work with community colleges and other organizations. Probably nothing describes my rigorous approach to grant writing more than a note from Julia Morrison at East Mississippi Community College in September 2020. It was addressed both to me and Dr. Raj Shaunak, her supervisor (excerpted):

> I am immensely grateful to you both for the time and interest you took in teaching me the basics of grant writing, aligning the proposal to strategic goals, developing a detailed and justified budget, and sourcing ample support letters. While I learned more than I could ever imagine from working with you both, chief among those lessons was watching Bill dissect the RFP [request for proposal] to ensure we covered all our bases.
>
> While I am not an expert grant writer by any stretch of the imagination, I owe any competency I might have to you both for your mentorship and tutoring. If Bill hadn't been so precise (read anal) about ensuring precision and forcing us to articulate the who, what, when, where, why, and most importantly HOW—I wouldn't have had any frame of reference for how to take mush and make it cohesive.
>
> This experience has made me so grateful for how Bill approached the process of grant writing. He didn't tolerate a lot of bullshit, which forced those who worked with him to clarify their objectives.

Another experience at The Montgomery Institute taught me quite different aspects of rigorous thinking. I became a certified instructor for Stephen Covey's *The 7 Habits of Highly Effective People*. While the whole methodology required serious thinking, Habits 1 and 5 helped frame useful rigorous thinking. The essence of Habit 1, "be proactive," is to think and consider before you react. The essence of Habit 5, "seek first to understand, then to be understood," is to put yourself in others' shoes before coming to conclusions. Such reflections provide understanding and insight and mitigate bias that are essential to useful thinking. My Habit 5 thinking caused some consternation among media friends, as related in my column "Uh Oh! An Idea Was Committed," reproduced above.

My greatest personal experience with rigorous, strategic thinking came during the 1991, 1993, and 1995 fights to save Naval Air Station Meridian from closure by the Defense Base Closure and Realignment Commission (BRAC). A group we called the Navy Meridian Team consisted of retired naval officers, base civilians, key civic leaders, and me as team leader. Jack Douglass, David Stevens, John Carrier, Sue Van Court,

Mike Reich, Brian Dabbs, Dr. Bill Scaggs, and I formed the core "war group." We quickly learned that the breadth and depth of data used by the navy to assess bases required a rigorous approach. The team worked day and night reviewing complex data calls, capacity charts, military value matrices, minutes of navy evaluation committees, COBRA cost projections, and economic impact data. We survived the first round in 1991. That strenuous experience helped the team become highly effective at its work. In 1993 and 1995, our rigorous approach led to discovering holes in the navy's arguments for closure. We were able to build detailed cases that refuted attacks by competing bases and the claims made by navy analysts. In the end, NAS Meridian was the only base in America to go through all three 1990s closure rounds and survive.

Despite these successes, other experiences with major community and regional development projects would teach me that rigorous thinking was only the first step toward solving deep-rooted problems. Such thinking had to be coupled with highly effective teams and sustained collaborative leadership.

HIGHLY EFFECTIVE TEAMS AND SUSTAINED COLLABORATIVE LEADERSHIP

You know that Yogi Berra saying, "When you come to the fork in the road, take it"? Well, I took a good number of them. Collectively they taught me the efficacy of thinking rigorously, the importance of highly effective teams and collaborative leadership, and the necessity for sustained leadership. They also revealed the complexities involved in dealing with our entrenched dilemmas.

Rigorous, strategic thinking and planning alone did not save NAS Meridian. It also required collaborative leadership from Representative G. V. "Sonny" Montgomery, Senators Thad Cochran and Trent Lott, Governors Ray Mabus and Kirk Fordice, and many local and state officials in combination with a highly effective Navy Meridian Team. Other communities with strong political connections lost bases when their cases could not hold up to rigorous scrutiny by the BRAC staff. The lesson was clear. Rigorous, strategic thinking forms the basis for solving difficult dilemmas. Collaborative leadership in combination with highly effective teams gets rigorous solutions implemented.

Team building for community initiatives occurred frequently during my thirty-eight-year relationship with Dr. William F. "Bill" Scaggs, the longtime president of Meridian Community College. There were teams he created, teams I helped him create, and teams he helped me create. Each successful initiative resulted from collaborative leadership and a highly effective team.

One was the Coalition for Good Government in 1988, which successfully replaced obstructionists on the Meridian City Council. Another was a team of bankers and economic developers that created the East Mississippi Development Corporation loan fund in 1989 to help start up minority businesses. A third was the Navy Meridian Team. A fourth was the broad community process in 1991 that led to combining the Meridian Chamber of Commerce, the Lauderdale Economic Development Authority (which I chaired), and the Lauderdale Tourism Commission into the Meridian–Lauderdale County Partnership.

There were more, one of which taught me a key lesson about how hard it is to reform school policy at the local level. High on pulling people together to form the Meridian–Lauderdale County Partnership, Bill and I thought we might pull community leaders together to improve schools. Bill, serving as partnership chairman, and I got *Meridian Star* editor Lloyd Gray to chair the partnership's special Education Task Force. (Years later, Lloyd would become executive director of the Phil Hardin Foundation.) We thought Lloyd would be seen as a neutral advocate for change. The key goal of the task force was to improve educational quality. The final report issued in October 1992 called for twelve changes in local education practices—one was a no pass/no play rule for athletics (read football). Deemed by partnership leaders as too controversial to pursue so soon after its formation, the report was never made public.

Rigorous thinking, highly effective teams, and collaborative leadership also worked to develop and implement the previously mentioned

Ford Foundation project, the Rural Community College Initiative (RCCI), from 1996 to 2000, fostering improvements in prenatal education, parental skill building, childhood readiness for school, elementary school reading and math, college developmental education, and community leadership training. It worked over that same period for development of the JumpStart Entrepreneur Development Program William Hatcher and I crafted with funding from the Ewing Marion Kauffman Foundation. In 2001, JumpStart was one of forty-three international programs recognized as a benchmark practice for local economies by the US secretaries of agriculture and education.

It worked similarly for the Workforce Innovation in Regional Economic Development project. From 2006 to 2010, team leaders engaged with 832 organizations and institutions; reached 8,857 individuals through community development planning and outreach activities; held community development charrettes in thirty-four communities; awarded 10,411 WorkKeys Career Readiness Certificates; provided unique local entrepreneur information cards to 158 communities; established free online access for advanced manufacturing and entrepreneur training; established new entrepreneur credit training classes and advanced manufacturing training classes at eight colleges; leveraged an additional $13 million in project support funding; and provided staff support for project activities in thirty-seven counties.

But these positive outcomes would fade years later because rigorous thinking, highly effective teams, and collaborative leadership needed one more thing for lasting impact—sustained leadership.

The Ford Foundation initiative had great potential to transform our community, but as college, school, and community leaders turned over, circumstances evolved, and external funding ended, commitments and priorities changed. Consequently, few of the programs were sustained. One exception was The Montgomery Institute (TMI), which was birthed by the project. When I retired in 2021, TMI had reinvented itself several times and was going strong. That success was due in large part to the sustained collaborative leadership provided by AT&T regional manager C. D. Smith, the institute's one and only chairman.

The Workforce Innovation in Regional Economic Development (WIRED) initiative had great potential to transform rural areas in east Mississippi and west Alabama, but as leadership and partners turned over and project funding ended, commitments to the project waned. The eight community college alliance dissolved. Entrepreneur services and training dwindled. College engagement in community development dropped off. Only some of the manufacturing training improvements were sustained, though at different levels. One major sustained success was advanced manufacturing training at East Mississippi Community College. Dr. Raj Shaunak took the work accomplished during WIRED and transformed the college's workforce training into a model program for the Southeast. It was remarkable demonstration of sustained collaborative leadership how Dr. Shaunak drew on the expertise of his team members and kindled their desire to do something extraordinary.

Frustratingly, I had found the lack of sustained leadership to be a key failing even for projects with rigorous thinking, collaborative leadership, and great teams. It was a hole in the whole at the state level, too.

SUSTAINED COLLABORATIVE LEADERSHIP IN STATE GOVERNMENT

With succor from Dr. Bill Scaggs and MSU professor Dr. Ned Lovell, I crafted a paradigm for highly effective team development. It featured rigorous, relevant, and righteous behavior driving four essential processes: (1) research, planning, and strategy development; (2) human, physical, and financial resource development; (3) collaborative and sustainable leadership development; and (4) internal and external relationship building. All these factors contributed to the Navy Meridian Team's success.

My research discovered few examples of sustained collaborative leadership in Mississippi state government.

Soon after his election as governor, William Winter created a Blue Ribbon Committee on Education made up of his appointees, legislators, and the state superintendent of education. Rigorous research by the committee led to twenty-three proposals that became Winter's proposed Education Reform Act in 1982. Most of the proposals died when he could not get the legislature to cooperate. It took Governor Winter working tirelessly hand in hand with educators and the Mississippi Economic Council (MEC) to fire up support and get a handful of key things approved—a constitutional referendum to put the Board of Education in and the elected superintendent out of the constitution, state funding for kindergartens, compulsory school attendance, school accountability, statewide testing, and teaching assistants. While these changes lasted, that intense support for education enhancements could not be sustained, particularly with regard to school funding. Similarly, Governor Ray Mabus could not get the legislature to fund his BEST school reform program, which included school performance incentives and sanctions, dropout prevention, adult literacy, and early childhood screening programs.

The MEC, composed of business leaders from around the state, was a major force for improvement in Mississippi, providing rigorous research and business leadership for numerous strategic efforts. Its challenge was to get and sustain collaborative leadership from the public sector. As noted, the MEC played a key role in getting William Winter's kindergarten program passed in 1982. Its members, led by former MEC president Owen Cooper, played a critical role in getting Mississippi's four-lane highway program Advocating Highways for Economic Advancement and Development (AHEAD) approved in 1987 (Gil Carmichael also played a leadership role). The influence of business leaders back then, compared to three decades later, was such that five of us six House Republicans helped pass a bill that increased gas taxes in an election year. It took an override of Governor Bill Allain's veto, which we passed by two votes.

In the final years of Governor Ronnie Musgrove's administration, the MEC in cooperation with universities initiated the major planning process called Blueprint Mississippi, chaired by Ole Miss chancellor Robert Khayat. Budget shortfalls and Hurricane Katrina would thwart most of its fifty-three key strategies from seeing the light of day. As

Haley Barbour's second term in office drew to a close in 2011, an effort to refresh Blueprint Mississippi emerged. This MEC effort chaired by IHL commissioner Hank Bounds had much less impact than the original Blueprint effort. The MEC could not get Governor Phil Bryant and other state leaders to fully engage in pursuing its goals. This effort reflected a weakening of the MEC's and business leaders' influence over government policy.

In late 2015, the MEC released its well-researched and documented Excelerate Mississippi study, a Blueprint outgrowth, showing the dire need to dramatically increase funding for highways and bridge repairs across the state. I wrote about this.

ROAD AND BRIDGE CRISIS CAUSES GREAT PONDERATION

January 19, 2017

Riding the rural highways of Mississippi, it is easy to see why so many citizens want taxes cut. Vistas of disrepair and deterioration overwhelm. Strapped folk in these areas see little benefit from state spending. To them, every precious dollar they send to state and local governments must seem to disappear down endless holes. They are beyond taxed enough already.

Now, these highways they depend on for work, church, and groceries have begun to buckle and crack. Bad roads will worsen their plight unless and until money is spent to fix them. But there is not enough money for repairs, especially for poor, rural areas. And there won't be without more tax revenues.

This infrastructure calamity has become a matter of great ponderation in Jackson.

Lt. Gov. Tate Reeves told a Stennis Institute gathering last week the matter is one legislators can't ignore, adding that road and bridge repair is a "core function" of government. True, so long as pondering is different from ignoring.

You see, legislators have known about, and pondered, this problem for years. Back in 2009, their own PEER Committee told them the backlog for just bridge repairs had grown to $975 million. Then, in 2013, PEER told them the bridge backlog had jumped to $2.7 billion. In 2015, the Mississippi Economic Council told them nearly $6 billion was needed to fix both bridges and highways.

Naturally, each bigger number created a need for greater ponderation.

Today, money needed to fix roads and bridges is nearing $7 billion.

Meanwhile, legislative leaders have a self-made dilemma. Back in 2015, business leaders warned them bad roads would hurt the state economy and asked them to raise taxes. Legislative leaders promised to take care of the issue. Instead, they've pondered.

This past summer, legislative leaders listened to their chosen tax consultant tell them user taxes should be the primary means of funding government functions. They liked what they heard.

Well, the gas tax is the user tax Mississippi levies to pay for roads and bridges. It was last increased in 1987. For years now, it has provided too little money to cover both new construction and repairs. The easy and, according to the tax consultant, proper fix would be to increase the gas tax.

Antitax rural folks have a different thought. They want tax cuts, not tax increases, not even just a few cents per gallon of gas. They don't get, or don't care, that good roads are essential for a good economy.

Meanwhile, roads and bridges deteriorate more each year, putting everyone's economic well-being at risk.

Impatient business leaders want legislative leaders to keep their promise. Republican legislators in control understand, but want to keep their jobs.

As drivers jerk and shudder down ever more rugged highways, they can rest assured of one thing. Mississippi's legislative leaders, like Pinky and the Brain, will ponder this matter with great deliberation.

PS—Reeves said possible help from Donald Trump's infrastructure plan would now be included in their ponderation.

Unlike in 1987, the MEC and business leaders were unable to get Governor Bryant, Lieutenant Governor Reeves, Speaker Gunn, or the majority of Republican legislators to collaborate on the needed funding mechanism. Plans for a fuel tax increase succumbed to growing antitax, antigovernment Tea Party sentiments. This failure further eroded the influence of the MEC and business leaders.

In fiscal years 2021, 2022, and 2023, the legislature did inject substantial funding into road and bridge repairs but still had not established an ongoing funding mechanism.

There was one highly successful initiative at the state level that utilized rigorous thinking, highly effective teams, and sustained collaborative leadership—Governor Haley Barbour's response and recovery initiative following the devastation from Hurricane Katrina in 2005. Haley's rigorously planned, assiduously implemented hurricane recovery and rebuild plan, chaired by business leader Jim Barksdale, achieved great success and appreciation. My role in this as deputy director at the MDA was limited, but I got to travel with Haley and observe much of the planning process. I also spent two weeks embedded in hard-hit Hancock County, where Katrina made landfall, helping to coordinate local recovery activities with the Federal Emergency Management Agency (FEMA) and the Mississippi Emergency Management Agency (MEMA). Haley well described the success of that initiative in his book *America's Great Storm: Leading through Hurricane Katrina*.

"There is a cycle of life to all places," I wrote in my 2010 award-winning treatise "Rural Place Building" after returning to The Montgomery Institute in 2008. "They build up, they decline. Great places learn to break the cycle . . . they preserve, they rebuild, they sustain. They grow and retain three types of civic leaders—entrepreneurs who see opportunities and seize them, stewards who manage already built good things and keep them viable and ever renewed, and champions who see to the leadership development and resource gathering needed to build and sustain vital programs over time." A big hole in the whole has been Mississippi's failure to develop and sustain such leadership at the state level.

My friend and entrepreneurship authority William Hatcher visited Haiti following a major earthquake. He was there on a church-sponsored mission trying to impact the "culture of poverty" that pervaded that country. "If you can't change the culture, you can't change anything," he explained, saying he saw the same problem in Mississippi. The Ford Foundation, Kellogg Foundation, and other foundations working in this arena say that cultural change is hard, takes generations, and requires committed leadership. A dynamic economy helps, too.

Most communities do not have a culture of leadership. Some do briefly but cannot sustain it. For example, over his twenty-five-year career as director of the Meridian Chamber of Commerce, Wilton J.

"Bill" Johnson created a culture of leadership. After I got active in 1980, that is where I learned about community leadership and got my first experiences as a community leader. However, that culture of leadership faded away after Bill retired.

THE TUPELO MODEL

"Learning when to hand off leadership and the willingness to hand off leadership are seasonings you see in only the finest community leadership recipes"—Ron Heifetz, author of "Leadership without Easy Answers."

I knew of only one success in regional and community development in Mississippi that utilized sustained collaborative leadership in combination with rigorous strategic thinking and highly effective teams. Vaughn Grisham Jr. wrote a book about it, *Tupelo: The Evolution of a Community*. It is the story of how Tupelo developed sustained, persistent, collaborative leadership that did its research, developed relevant and mutually beneficial strategies, gathered necessary resources, and pulled the segments of their community together behind a common purpose. I wrote about this.

IF ONLY TUPELO'S UNIFYING CULTURE REACHED STATEWIDE

January 20, 2018

Do you know the Tupelo Story, the uplifting chronicle of Tupelo's self-transformation from "a hardscrabble hamlet" (Aspen Institute) to a prosperous small city and "national model for homegrown development" (William Winter)?

Vaughn Grisham Jr. built a career around telling the Tupelo Story and was the founding director of the McLean Institute for Public Service and Community Engagement at Ole Miss. His book, *Tupelo: The Evolution of a Community*, tells the story, as does his monograph with Rob Gurwitt, "Hand in Hand: Community Economic Development in Tupelo," a case study published by the Aspen Institute.

In the foreword to Grisham's book, former governor William Winter calls Tupelo "a place where people have learned not to dismiss their own personal self-interest, but to equate it with the interest of their community."

While *Daily Journal* publisher George McLean was the enlightened self-interest guru and unrelenting catalyst behind Tupelo's transformation, the Tupelo Story is really a multigenerational story of strong and progressive business leadership, inclusive community engagement, well-researched and strategic decisions, and institutionalized civic processes.

I was reminded of the story by a *Daily Journal* editorial last week entitled "Continued Community Success Depends on Training Next Generation." It told of the Tupelo mayor's Youth Council leadership program teaching youth the Tupelo Story and inspiring them to "continue the history of engaged and dedicated leadership our community has benefited from for the past seventy-five years."

You see, what Tupelo has developed is a unifying "community culture" (Grisham) that intentionally renews itself, edifies its business and community leaders, and thereby sustains the city's focus on helping both its people and its businesses do better.

In looking to answer why Mississippi persistently ranks at the bottom in so many indicators, you need look no further than to our lack of a vibrant, unifying state culture. Unlike Tupelo, we have been unable to bridge divisions rooted in race, provincialism, self-interest, and ideology. Thus, instead of discourse leading to success and distinction, we get unending squabbles that foster distress, disappointment, dysfunction, distrust, and discombobulation.

Nothing is more symptomatic of this condition than the rank partisanship in our state legislature. Indeed, its leaders tout partisanship and offer no proposals to bridge divisions and develop a unifying culture.

Tupelo ensconced its forward-looking business leadership in its Community Development Foundation (CDF). Not satisfied with the chamber of commerce model, McLean designed the CDF to serve the full community along with business interests.

The only organization to come close to the CDF at the state level has been the Mississippi Economic Council (MEC). While primarily business focused, the MEC, like the CDF, has championed education, health care, and other quality-of-life initiatives. But despite ambitious efforts like Blueprint Mississippi, the MEC has been unable to forge sufficient consensus to bridge the state's many divisions.

Lately, MEC influence has dwindled as that of antiprogressive out-of-state special interest groups has surged.

It is human nature to put self-interest first. Once George McLean convinced Tupelo business leaders that balancing self-interest with community interests would be better for all, the city and region prospered. Tupelo has carefully nurtured this approach through future generations of business and community leadership.

How far off the bottom might Mississippi be if this approach had reached statewide?

Grisham maintained that "institutionalized civic structures" were crucial to Tupelo's success. He described his story as a "tale of citizens bonding together into a community." He said that it "chronicles what is possible when community is achieved and people learn to work toward common goals." One leader after another sustained the rigorous thinking and collaborative approach McLean established. Two decades after McLean's death, I would take participants in Leadership Lauderdale from Meridian to Tupelo to hear successors like Jack Reed tell their unique story.

I knew of one other similar community success resulting from sustained collaborative leadership. But it was not in Mississippi. It happened in the unlikeliest of places, impoverished Clarke County in the Alabama Black Belt. The Montgomery Institute worked with Thomasville during the WIRED grant as well as through a program called Educating Artists and Entrepreneurs to Build Creative Economies in Rural Areas. Mayor Sheldon Day, a former Walmart store manager, also was a key member of TMI's West Alabama–East Mississippi Mayors Network. I wrote about Day's efforts.

DAY SHOWS RURAL COMMUNITIES CAN SUCCEED

March 16, 2017

Rural communities in the South can succeed.

Thomasville, a small town in Alabama's poor "Black Belt," has thrived under the leadership of Mayor Sheldon Day. Indeed, Day has his folks believing it is "cool to be rural."

Census data shows Thomasville with 4,209 residents and a low family poverty rate of 13% compared to 25% for the whole of Clarke County and 19% for Alabama. The town's poverty rate has been in steep decline since 2010, as median household income jumped 28% from $28,234 to $36,146.

The five-hundred-student Thomasville High School, with 48% minority students and 63% who qualify for free and reduced lunches, boasts a stellar graduation rate of 95%.

During his twenty years as mayor, Day has attracted over $700 million in capital investments and increased the number of industrial parks from one to five. He estimated that 50% of the businesses along the Highway 43 bypass in Thomasville have opened during his tenure, and sales tax collections have tripled.

In 2013, Thomasville beat sixty-two other sites to secure the $100 million Golden Dragon Precise Copper Tubing facility, the first major manufacturer from China to locate in Alabama.

Day is especially proud of the partnership he built among the high school, Alabama Southern Community College, and industries. The dual enrollment program he championed in welding fourteen years ago now includes industrial maintenance, information technology, pre-engineering, pre-nursing and sports medicine.

"Today there are more dual enrollment high school students at the Thomasville campus than regular students on Alabama Southern's main campus in Monroeville," Day said. Coupled with an intensive work-based learning program at the high school, the dual enrollment program, Day says, has been a "major catalyst to attract industry."

Fascinated by his success, Betsy Rowell, executive director of the Stone County [Mississippi] Economic Development Partnership, invited Day to tour her county and speak at her annual meeting. "He has obviously had great success with partnerships in his area. Our local leadership needed to hear his message."

How is Thomasville succeeding in an area where most rural towns struggle?

Day said when he was first elected mayor in 1996 he spent time searching out the best models for rural development. He found that model in Tupelo. He studied Tupelo and became a disciple of Vaughn Grisham, director emeritus of the McLean Institute for Public Service and Community Engagement at the University of Mississippi.

Day points to several similarities. One is the broad cooperative spirit he has nurtured. "In Thomasville, the school, chamber, industry, and city are all partners," he says. "Everybody talks to each other to get things done." Another has been his intense focus on developing the local workforce. And, like Tupelo did with Toyota, he collaborated with an adjacent county, Wilcox, to create an industrial park to locate a major industry. Now, he is copying Tupelo's health care model and will soon build a new regional hospital.

No longer the student, he now lectures on how to succeed in rural communities at Auburn University's Economic Development Institute.

"His insight was invaluable," said Rowell.

In 2022, Sheldon had entered his twenty-sixth year as mayor. Whether Thomasville can sustain its culture of leadership post-Sheldon remains to be seen.

What Mississippi has lacked that these two towns have not has been strong, sustained, persistent, collaborative, trustworthy leadership. It takes that to develop a citizenry willing to be led. While we have not had such sustained unifying leadership at the state level, that does not mean we cannot.

SUMMARY

Solving Mississippi's many complex dilemmas would require rigorous thinking, highly effective teams, and sustained collaborative leadership. Governor Haley Barbour's successful recovery and rebuild plan after

Katrina utilized rigorous thinking, highly effective teams, and sustained collaborative leadership for the duration of the implementation period. Few other development initiatives, local or state, did. Only one, the Tupelo model, effectively practiced them all over many years.

Tupelo's approach to problem solving also modeled the good government approach as conservative, forward-thinking business leaders drove the process.

Chapter Six

A LINGERING HOPE AND A PRAYER

CONSTRUCTIVE "GOOD GOVERNMENT" CONSERVATISM

Mississippi and America have fallen prey to something founding father James Madison predicted. In "Federalist no. 10," published on November 23, 1787, Madison wrote about "factions" and their ability to thwart good government. By "faction," Madison meant a cluster of citizens "united and actuated by some common impulse of passion, or of interest, adverse to the rights of other citizens, or to the permanent and aggregate interests of the community." He considered the rise and fall of factions an inescapable problem. "So strong is this propensity of mankind to fall into mutual animosities, that where no substantial occasion presents itself, the most frivolous and fanciful distinctions have been sufficient to kindle their unfriendly passions and excite their most violent conflicts."

Our state political system was not designed for sustained leadership. Outside of government, strong, constructive business leadership with statewide influence has not been sustained. No influential civic or educational institutions have provided sustained constructive leadership statewide. In a state bogged down by aginner sentiments from the commingling of our shadows of cultural hatred, too many self-important peckerwoods of both races, and insane political behaviors, it became problematic to seek, much less build, consensus. Well-funded, intentionally biased, social and think tank structures formed to promote distorted truths. Their associated truth managers began to dominate political discussion. State politics became more aligned with national politics, fostering destructive factionalism rather than constructive consensus. Both Republicans and Democrats were guilty. Consequently, holes in the whole went unfilled and prolonged Mississippi's enduring grip on the bottom.

A political gambit in 2021 illustrates the aginner influence at the top levels of government. In his 2021 speech at the Neshoba County Fair, House Speaker Philip Gunn joined Governor Tate Reeves in expressing disdain for creeping socialism in government, a favorite aginner mantra, but a deceitful mantra. Jamie Dimon, one of America's great capitalists and head of America's largest bank, JP Morgan Chase, took issue with the aginner mantra. In a 2019 stockholder report, Dimon contended we should focus more on fixing capitalism than on fearing socialism. "There is no question that capitalism has been the most successful economic system the world has ever seen," he said. "This is not to say that capitalism does not have flaws, that it isn't leaving people behind and that it shouldn't be improved."

"Simply put, the social needs of far too many of our citizens are not being met," he concluded.

Dimon's view echoed that of Scottish politician and journalist Noel Skelton in 1923. Concerned about growing dissatisfaction with conservatism in England, Skelton penned four articles in April and May 1923 under the heading "Constructive Conservatism" that challenged conservatives to adapt to the growing appeal of socialism. I wrote about that.

CONSTRUCTIVE CONSERVATISM NEEDED TO THWART RISE OF SOCIALISM

February 9, 2019

What would Adam Smith, the father of modern capitalism, think of capitalism in America today?

You see, it was Smith's notion that despite natural greed, individuals in a free, capitalistic society would be led by "reason, principle, [and] conscience" to act morally and compassionately. Capitalism would be the economic mechanism by which wage earners and the middle class would accumulate wealth. While certainly true historically in the United States and much of the free world, that no longer seems to be the case here, especially since the Great Recession.

> "Only upper-income families have median wealth greater than prior to the Great Recession." —Pew Research Center, November 1, 2017

> "The income share of the poorest half of Americans is declining while the richest have grabbed more. In Europe, it's not happening." —Vox, July 29, 2018

> "The US Congressional Research Service says the income share of the richest 1% of Americans reached 19.6% last year. It never rose above 10% in the first four decades after the Second Word War." —*Telegraph*, February 5, 2019

And, so what, you say?

"According to a new poll from Gallup, young Americans are souring on capitalism. Less than half, 45%, view capitalism positively," CNBC reported last August. "Meanwhile, 51% of young people are positive about socialism."

Perhaps you noticed the leftward swing in the midterm elections last year. According to Axios, "The Democratic Party's base is rallying around calls for massive social welfare programs like Medicare for All, a federal jobs guarantee, and a Green New Deal—all of which would cost trillions of dollars and potentially bust the budget," which they say "is not that big of a deal."

This trend is not new. In 2011, BBC News Magazine published an article that declared, "As a side-effect of the financial crisis, more and more people are starting to think Karl Marx was right."

To counter this trend, what have conservatives done? So far, they continue to promote rapacious capitalism, facilitate corporate greed, and provide fuel to energize the left.

In 1923, Scottish politician and journalist Noel Skelton penned a series of antisocialism articles challenging fellow conservatives to step up and face the social and economic challenges facing his nation. He called this approach "constructive progressive conservatism" and said that growing the wealth of wage earners through fair wages and property ownership should be conservatives' top priority to thwart the appeal of socialism.

In today's parlance, that means big business should be hiring more people and increasing wages rather than funding stock buybacks, creating expensive mergers, and escalating corporate salaries (now 270 times average wage-earner salaries, up from 20 times in 1970). Crumbs to the middle class from massive tax cuts for huge corporations and the wealthy and low-wage jobs with no benefits and no future won't dent the rise of socialism.

So, who are the champions of constructive conservatism in America today?

Well, John Kasich, former governor of Ohio, may come closest. Quoting conservative Catholic philosopher Michael Novak, he said capitalism without compassion is "bankrupt."

An ironic call for "moral capitalism" to combat socialism comes from Rep. Joe Kennedy (yes, one of those Kennedys). "We have to do a better job addressing the economic needs of working-class and middle-class voters," he told the Associated Press.

Some form of constructive conservatism will be needed to thwart the rise of socialism.

Gil Carmichael and Haley Barbour saw a limited role for government that could, and should, adapt to growing social needs. Their constructive "good government" conservative view of government functions allowed for that. To varying extents, that was also the view and approach of former president Ronald Reagan and Republican governors of Ohio, Tennessee, Florida, Indiana, Iowa, Texas, Arkansas, Nevada, New Mexico, South Dakota, and North Carolina—John Kasich, Lamar Alexander, Jeb Bush, Mike Pence, Terry Branstad, George W. Bush, Asa Hutchinson, Brian Sandoval, Susana Martinez, Dennis Daugaard, and Jim Martin, respectively. The good government notion here does not advocate the liberal view of big government, but a conservative view of limited government adapting to evolving dilemmas to solve problems.

"Today's Republican Party and its candidates are stuck in a trap of orthodoxy, a paralyzing fear of stepping out of line and doing or saying anything that might upset their noisy party mates who can't see past Trumpian dogma," wrote Kasich in a January 2023 article for *Time* magazine. "Unable to look at problems in a new way with constructive policies and solutions, they bring only anger, resentment, and intolerance to the table. It's a tiresome and ultimately losing platform based on being against anything the Democrats are for, mixed with intolerance of anyone different from themselves.

"The party has forgotten what it means to be a compassionate conservative or how to address issues by observing those underlying, faith-based values that once formed the core of what it means to be a Republican," Kasich continued.

It is significant to note that the good government conservatives mentioned above were leaders influenced by their faith. Jesus was not a socialist, yet he consistently called on us to help the poor. There are hundreds of places in the Bible that tell us how to treat with the poor. And nothing prohibits us from using government as a means to do so. Indeed, texts in Matthew 25 and Psalm 72 suggest a role for government.

Good government conservatism would guide that role. It adheres to the principles of reduced spending and limited government while also adhering to the principle that government has some responsibility for addressing the dilemmas of the poor.

TRIUMVIRATE OF POLICY POWER

There are the cold-hearted and the warm-hearted, the kind-hearted and the cruel-hearted, the soft-hearted and the hard-hearted among us. Do hearts matter when it comes to leadership?

Republicans' reluctance to pursue good government solutions to Mississippi's dilemmas constituted a major hole in the whole. In 2023, two-thirds of the Republican-controlled triumvirate of policy power in Mississippi—the governor, lieutenant governor, and speaker of the house—opposed constructive approaches to solving our dilemmas. House Speaker Philip Gunn and Governor Tate Reeves lined up on the antigovernment side, leaving Lieutenant Governor Delbert Hosemann alone on the good government side. Had retired Supreme Court justice Bill Waller Jr. won GOP nomination for governor in 2019, he would have shifted the balance of triumvirate power. He exhibited the heart and the wisdom needed to provide constructive leadership. But his late entry into the race—he waited until his Supreme Court term ended to get in—left him too far behind to catch up to Lieutenant Governor Tate Reeves.

I wrote about potential changes to the triumvirate of policy power in June 2023.

VOTERS COULD CHANGE TRIUMVIRATE OF POWER

June 4, 2023

Books, briefs, broadcasts, and blogs provide discourses galore on the growing concentration of wealth and power in America. Mississippi is not estranged from this trend. The transmogrification of the triumvirate of power that controls public policy and spending provides a good illustration.

The state constitution created this triumvirate by providing for a governor, a House of Representatives, and a Senate. By design, the governor is a singular power. In contrast, the House and Senate were designed to have power distributed among all their elected members.

Specifically, Section 38 provides that both the House and Senate "shall elect [their] own officers," and Section 55 provides that both "may determine rules of [their] own proceedings."

The constitution does not convey any significant legislative powers to the lieutenant governor, providing only that he or she serves as "president of the Senate." The constitution also does not create the position of or convey significant legislative powers to the speaker of the house. MS Code Section 5-1-11 does require the House to elect "a speaker."

The concentration of power that we now see in the offices of the speaker of the house and lieutenant governor has accrued over time through rules adopted by the members of the House and Senate. Those rules give the Speaker and lieutenant governor their mechanisms of power—authority to refer bills and appoint all committee chairs (except the president pro tempore chairs the Senate Rules Committee).

We have had powerful speakers and lieutenant governors who strongly influenced legislation in the past. But strong influence morphed into autocratic control during the reigns of Philip Gunn and Tate Reeves, as party politics became dominant. That trend has continued for the most part through Delbert Hosemann's term as lieutenant governor.

Thus, the triumvirate of power has essentially come to consist of three individuals, not one individual plus two bodies with distributed power.

Getting to the point of all this, the triumvirate will change next year.

We know the house speaker will change. Philip Gunn did not seek reelection. His replacement will be elected by the House in January. State Rep. Jason White, currently the house speaker pro tempore, is favored in that election.

This August, Lt. Gov. Hosemann faces a notable challenger in the Republican primary in State Sen. Chris McDaniel. In the November general election, Gov. Tate Reeves will likely face a notable Democratic challenger in Northern District Public Service Commissioner Brandon Presley.

The winners will wield immense power over state policy and spending if rank-and-file legislators continue to yield up that power. Voters should let legislative candidates know whether they are comfortable with such concentration of power or not.

"Don't be tyrants, but lead them by your good example." —1 Peter 5:3

Having one-third of the triumvirate pushing a constructive approach from 2020 through 2023 was at least heartening if not overwhelmingly beneficial.

In 2022, Lieutenant Governor Hosemann appointed a Senate Study Group on Women, Children, and Families to undertake a rigorous review of issues affecting children aged one to three. For the first time since Republicans took control, a legislative committee streamed professionals' presentations on issues affecting the state's bottom rankings on infant mortality, births to unwed mothers, low birth-weight babies, preterm births, and more. Few of the committee's recommendations passed the 2023 legislature. However, three successes were significant—extending postpartum Medicaid coverage from sixty days to twelve months; establishing an Early Intervention Task Force to Study the IDEA Part C Early Intervention System in Mississippi and Mississippi's Laws Regarding Early Intervention; and increasing Department of Health funding for early intervention by $2 million.

In 2023, Speaker Gunn announced he would not seek reelection to the House. In early 2024, Speaker Pro Tempore Jason White was elected speaker and moved into the triumvirate of power. Many saw White as more open to good government conservatism than Gunn. His initial statements as speaker suggested that was the case as he urged his colleagues to keep an "open mind" about health care and other issues. I mentioned White's approach to health care in a September 2023 column reiterating our dilemmas.

DO YOU WONDER WHY MISSISSIPPI HAS THE HIGHEST DEATH RATE?

September 10, 2023

A September 4 article in the *Atlantic* claimed that Republican politicians across the nation are "impoverishing and immiserating their own constituents" to gain political points with conservative voters.

It left out a key point. Some constituents have it worse.

Do you ever wonder why Mississippi has the highest death rate and the lowest life expectancy among the fifty states?

Surely you recall information emerging from the legislature earlier this year about Mississippi's highest-in-the-nation death rates for infants and pregnant moms.

Perhaps you remember two years ago in September 2021 when Mississippi surpassed New Jersey for the highest rate of COVID-19 deaths. "Since the start of the pandemic, at least 9,165 people in Mississippi have died of the virus," reported the Associated Press. "The state has a population of roughly three million and has had one of the worst vaccination rates in the country."

Mississippi also has the highest rates for several health-related causes of death—cancer, stroke, high blood pressure, kidney disease, and influenza/pneumonia. Plus the highest mortality rate from Alzheimer's disease and the second-highest for diabetes.

Then there are homicides—the latest data on homicide death rates ranked Mississippi at the top. We also have one of the highest rates for deaths in prison and the highest for deaths by firearms.

And car deaths—the most recent data shows Mississippi with the highest automobile fatality rate.

Back to the *Atlantic*'s contention. Are Mississippi politicians causing these constituent deaths? Not directly. But they are not preventing many of them. And that is a sobering takeaway.

It is no secret that more and better access to affordable health care would save many lives in Mississippi, from infants and pregnant moms to senior citizens with multiple morbidities. But rather than adopt and fund a constructive plan to address these issues, politicians over the years focused on tax cuts and budget cuts while allowing our health care infrastructure to wither when we needed it to be robust.

It is also no secret that greater investments in law enforcement at the local and state levels, including prisons, could reduce homicides, youth violence, and fatal traffic accidents. For example, the state expansion of the Capitol Police Force appears to have noticeably reduced homicides in Jackson.

Another thing the *Atlantic* article contends is that Republican politicians fail to invest in many such initiatives because "the prospective beneficiaries are less well-off and thus have less political influence."

But now comes a potential bright spot. Likely new speaker Jason White told Mississippi Today last week that he wants the House to look into all facets of health care.

"Let us not love with words or speech but with action and truth." —1 John 3:18

Having two-thirds of the triumvirate of power open to such a good government approach could greatly improve Mississippi's chances to close holes in the whole and lift our state off the bottom. But even if the triumvirate of policy power were unified in its commitment to pursue such a constructive course, overcoming Mississippi's shadows and the popularity of truth managers would take an eruption of good government champions across the state. Where would such champions come from?

CHANGING ATTITUDES

I want to talk to you today about this cobblestone. I found it in a large ramp beside the river Elbe in Dresden, Germany. I have no idea how old this piece of cobblestone is. But when I look at it, I wonder, did Martin Luther walk on it in 1517 on his way to incite the Reformation at the palace chapel? Did the fine Arabian stallion Marengo prance on it in 1813 as Napoleon celebrated his victory in the Battle of Dresden, one of his last before Waterloo? Did the renowned composer Richard Wagner stroll on it in the early nineteenth century?

Of course, if you're a cobblestone, you experience the grand occasionally and the less-than-grand every day. So, no doubt, over the years flocks, herds, droves, prides, teams, gaggles (this is the agriculturally correct part of my speech), and other such groups have, eh, perfumed and stepped on this piece of cobblestone with regularity.

After you leave here today and get on with your life, what will you become? Will you become a Martin Luther, a Napoleon, a Wagner? Or, will you settle for being a cobblestone in the highway of life?

(Excerpts from May 2021 commencement remarks at Mississippi State University.)

One hopeful sign for constructive change occurred when legislators voted to change the state flag in 2020. For years, Republican candidates had used opposition to changing the flag as a popular election message, a clear vestige of Faulkner's curse. Despite intense national pressure to change the flag, including pushes from the National Collegiate Athletic Association (NCAA) and Southeastern Conference, it looked like most Republican politicians would stay bowed up. That changed when faith leaders got behind making a change. I wrote about this in 2017 and 2020.

STATE FLAG CONFLICT: MORALITY VS. HERITAGE

September 23, 2017
(Excerpted)

Former state GOP executive director, elected Republican official, and chief of staff to Kirk Fordice, Mississippi's first Republican governor, Andy Taggart has publicly challenged his party to step up and "lead the charge in finally removing from our state flag the representation of the Confederate battle flag."

Saying such a move "will make a strong, moral statement" acknowledging that "our current state flag is divisive and hurtful to a significant number of our fellow Mississippians," Taggart joins Republican Speaker of the House Philip Gunn in taking a stand against the controversial flag.

"Changing the flag is the right thing to do," Speaker Gunn said last year. "We can deal with it now or leave it for future generations to address. I believe our state needs to address it now."

Over a decade ago, another longtime Republican leader spoke out strongly on racism, retired federal judge Charles Pickering.

All active Baptists, these three leaders align with the moral approach against racism pursued by the Southern Baptist Convention. In its historic resolution on racial reconciliation adopted in 1995, convention members resolved to "commit ourselves to be doers of the Word (James 1:22) by pursuing racial reconciliation in all our relationships, especially with our brothers and sisters in Christ (1 John 2:6), to the end that our light would so shine before others, that they may see [our] good works and glorify [our] Father in heaven (Matthew 5:16)."

Last year, the convention encouraged members to stop displaying the Confederate flag.

And this past June, the convention called every form of racism "antithetical to the Gospel of Jesus Christ" and resolved that "we still must make progress in rooting out any remaining forms of intentional or unintentional racism in our midst."

Taggart was lambasted in political blogs but garnered some praise for putting morality ahead of heritage regarding the flag conflict.

Where there is faith, there is hope.

FAITH PLAYS KEY ROLE IN CHANGING STATE FLAG

July 4, 2020

The Mississippi legislature plowed new ground last week when members heroically voted to banish the Confederate battle flag from the state flag, uprooting a longtime symbolic vestige of our segregationist past.

The unexpected success resulted from a rare convergence of liberal, conservative, business, and religious groups who provided resources, strategic messaging, and influencers to get the job done.

Think about it. Just getting to consider the bill to replace the flag took a two-thirds vote to suspend the rules in the Mississippi House and Senate, where conservative Republicans hold supermajorities. The key votes were 84 to 35 in the House and 36 to 14 in the Senate. The actual bill to change the flag passed 91 to 23 and 37 to 14.

It also took those two-thirds majority votes to get a reluctant Gov. Tate Reeves to agree to withhold a veto.

Speaker of the House Philip Gunn, who called for a flag change in 2015 and authored the final bill, and Lt. Gov. Delbert Hosemann played key roles. Other leaders and organizations outside government stepped up. Then, there was former governor Phil Bryant, who set the stage for this momentous success.

The resolution to suspend the rules stated: "To provide that the design for the Mississippi state flag recommended by the commission shall not include the design of the confederate battle flag, but shall include the words 'In God We Trust.'"

As far back as 2001, then State Auditor Bryant began to push "In God We Trust" into Mississippi's public arena. In 2014 as governor he got the phrase added to the state seal, which he put as the centerpiece of the bicentennial flag. In 2018, he approved putting the seal on Mississippi license plates. As Republican leaders began speaking out to change the flag, they also called for the replacement to be the "Seal" flag, a design featuring the state seal, rather than the popular "Stennis" or "Magnolia" flags.

Because of Bryant, the brilliant political move to propose swapping the battle flag for "In God We Trust" as the crux of the state flag was possible.

In Mississippi, faith still resonates more than other convictions. So, a flag proclaiming Mississippians' abiding faith could overcome allegiance to one proclaiming a divisive heritage.

On Tuesday before the crucial votes were cast, as reported in Mississippi Today, Gunn and Hosemann met with leaders representing many faiths. Soon afterward, the Mississippi Baptist Convention proclaimed support for a new flag. The Reverend Ligon Duncan, former senior pastor at the First Presbyterian Church in Jackson and now chancellor of Reformed Theological Seminary, called on legislators to "vote to take down the flag and replace it with a symbol that unites us all." Other pastors spread the word.

Days later, enough votes changed to change history.

"Behold, how good and pleasant it is when brothers dwell in unity." —Psalm 133:1

Make no mistake about it, changing the state flag represented a landmark change in attitudes for Mississippi. If attitudes on the state flag could change, so too could attitudes on other dilemmas with roots in our racist past—which would be a good many of the dilemmas that hold Mississippi to the bottom. Imagine a Mississippi where an additional 10 percent to 20 percent of the population worked and earned living wages. Over time, that is a goal good government conservatives could attain.

Regrettably, in 2023 too many in Mississippi, including our last two governors and most legislative leaders, bought into the antigovernment creed pushed by the voices of destructive factionalism. That made my hope that most of Mississippi's faithful would choose a constructive and limited government role in solving our dilemmas difficult if not unlikely. Such thinking always seemed schizophrenic, if not dubious, to me, given the reliance on God in the founding of our country, something I also wrote about.

WITHOUT CREATOR, CAN MEN BE CREATED EQUAL?

June 24, 2016

Next week we celebrate our founding fathers' 1776 decision to declare independence from England. In so doing, they laid down the principles that would guide the new nation. Their Declaration of Independence began:

"We hold these truths to be self-evident, that all men are created equal, that they are endowed by their Creator with certain unalienable Rights, that among these are Life, Liberty and the pursuit of Happiness. That to secure these rights, Governments are instituted among Men, deriving their just powers from the consent of the governed."

By 1789, our founding fathers had drafted, and the states ratified, a unique constitution based on the Declaration's principles, a constitution embracing government by the people and designed to forever secure their Creator-endowed rights.

In writing the Declaration, Thomas Jefferson drew heavily from John Locke's Second Treatise of Government wherein the English physician turned political philosopher cited God-made natural law to assert that all men are created equal, the only legitimate governments are those that have the consent of the people, and "no one ought to harm another in his life, health, liberty, or possessions."

Throughout the start-up of the new nation, our founding fathers sought the favor of their Creator. For example, the Continental Congress in 1782 put on the Great Seal of the United States the inscription "Annuit Coeptis," meaning that he (God) has favored our undertakings. In 1789, George Washington gave his First Inaugural Address, saying therein, "No people can be bound to acknowledge and adore the Invisible Hand which conducts the affairs of men more than those of the United States."

Reflect on this heritage. Then, consider where we are today.

Many think our government now rejects the notion of a Creator. Why else, they say, are "God" and "Creator" wiped from school textbooks and religious expressions ousted from public places? How else can biblical concepts of marriage and perversion be upended by a government instituted to secure Creator-endowed rights?

Indeed, it has become politically incorrect to side with the Bible, ironically the holy book most federal officials swear on when they take an oath to uphold the constitution.

If we allow our government to reject the notion of a Creator, what, then, becomes of the principles underlying our constitution: Creator-endowed rights and all men created equal?

Some say liberty, alone, is a sufficient principle. But, as Locke asserted and Alexis de Tocqueville affirmed, "liberty cannot be established without morality, nor morality without faith." History shows that liberty unconstrained by morality decays into indulgence and depravity.

Some say such decay is well underway with our rampant pornography, sex, and associated diseases; predatory abuse; epidemic lawlessness and senseless murders; unconstrained greed; and so on.

"I have a dream," said Martin Luther King Jr., "that one day this nation will rise up and live out the true meaning of its creed: 'We hold these truths to be self-evident; that all men are created equal.'"

Lacking a Creator or creed, we have no up to rise to. This July Fourth, pray for our nation.

Conservative-minded people of faith who follow Jesus and care about the left out and left behind would be the likely source for good government champions. Getting them to challenge popular antigovernment concepts and step into our caustic public arena would be daunting. Yet, that should be a key mission for our many good souls and others among the faithful. Only a union of constructive political leadership and champions from the faithful will lift Mississippi up.

My hope that the faithful will eventually come around relies on Romans 14:19, which tells us to "pursue what makes for peace and for mutual upbuilding" (ESV).

A PATH FROM THE BOTTOM

"What has been the principal lesson of a life spent in politics, business, and public service?" Sid Salter asked. *"The principal lesson I've learned is that progress is a twelve-letter word spelled p-e-r-s-e-v-e-r-a-n-c-e. The hardest lesson I've learned (some say still learning) is the patience to persevere with a good will. My role model was Sonny Montgomery."*

Mississippi's chances to rise from the bottom would be greatly enhanced by changed attitudes and good government leadership. But, as the Tupelo model taught us, sustained constructive change would also require Tupelo-style leadership and civic structures at the state, regional, and local levels. Fortunately, many structures exist that could be tapped.

Our universities in coordination with organizations like the Mississippi Economic Council could provide reliable rigorous thinking and data analysis about our bottom-hugging issues. That combination functioned well in providing policy analysis and research for Blueprint Mississippi. But that effort was temporary. A more permanent consortium would be needed. A useful model would be the Rural Policy Research Institute, a multistate interdisciplinary research consortium based out of the University of Missouri.

A number of structures exist that could provide the means for diverse leaders across the state to meet regularly to review the research, craft regional and statewide strategies, and identify available resources. For example, the state's ten planning and development districts must craft regional Comprehensive Economic Development Strategy (CEDS) plans at least every five years to qualify for federal Economic Development Administration assistance under its Public Works and Economic Adjustment Assistance programs. But these tend to be one-time, perfunctory, inward-looking efforts every five years. As Harry Martin, the highly successful Tupelo developer, told me, "In the South we tend to get together and pool our ignorance rather than finding outsiders who have answers." The process would need to be more like the CREATE Foundation's seventeen-county Commission on the Future of Northeast Mississippi. The commission meets annually, holds quarterly development roundtables, draws on outside research and expertise, and crafts regional goals and initiatives. Ideas and strategies get pushed down to local chambers of commerce and economic development agencies for discussion and implementation.

A process for collaborative leaders to emerge would be necessary, leaders able to bring together and manage highly effective teams to implement identified strategies. Economic developer Gray Swoope taught me that strong business leadership committed to making a difference is crucial to sustaining community development efforts. It takes such commitment to bring diverse interests together, face facts, find common ground, forge common vision, and prepare communities for change. In Tupelo, the Community Development Foundation and the CREATE Foundation served as the driving organizations to gather such leaders and to provide ongoing structural support and coordination. Organizations like the Mississippi Economic Council and one or more major philanthropic organizations could serve as driving organizations for a statewide initiative.

Sustaining research and leadership structures while also sustaining implementation efforts for a generation or more would be the ultimate challenge. But that would become likely to occur once initial structures began operating and showing progress.

CONCLUSION

In this era when the American way of life is threatened in so many ways, those who commit their time and make sacrifices for the betterment of their community are modern-day American patriots.

Gil Carmichael had a vision for good government to lift Mississippi off the bottom. Haley Barbour had a pragmatic plan to move Mississippi up. But the modern Republican Party they helped build abandoned their constructive objectives for starve-the-beast and tax-cut agendas. As a consequence, holes in the whole that existed when Democrats controlled state government have persisted under Republican control. Mississippi has continued to hug the bottom in state rankings, with large numbers of left out and left behind citizens.

My lifelong dream was that my Republican Party would pry Mississippi off the bottom. That did not occur. Now, at the end of my journey, I am left with but a lingering hope that such might happen. That hope was fueled by the changed attitudes exhibited in the successful initiative to change the state flag along with constructive policies and rigorous thinking championed by good government conservatives like Lieutenant Governor Delbert Hosemann and new Speaker of the House Jason White.

If good government conservatives could take charge, the ingredients exist to close our holes in the whole and end our enduring distress. The Tupelo model illustrates how to harness rigorous strategic thinking, highly effective teams, and sustained collaborative leadership. Our universities in coordination with organizations like the Mississippi Economic Council could provide reliable rigorous thinking and data analysis about our bottom-hugging issues. Studies like the Cycle of Prosperity benchmarks show the policy areas that must be addressed. An abundance of good souls stand available to provide leadership and manpower when given the opportunity.

But no good government leadership will gain full control over the triumvirate of policy power until the faithful make it happen. In my view, no other group, alliance, or institution remained sufficiently influential in 2023 to force such a change.

My lingering hope leads me to conclude with this prayer:

Lord, in accordance with your teachings, I pray you will cause more attitudes to change among your faithful so that they will support limited government actions to improve conditions for our left out and left behind. I pray you will bring forth champions from our abundance of good souls to lead a flag-like movement to pry Mississippi off the bottom. And I pray you will guide those champions to put in place the structures needed to sustain improvements over time. Amen.

As J. P. said in the movie *Angels in the Outfield* while looking to the heavens, "It could happen."

ACKNOWLEDGMENTS

I wish to thank Craig Gill, Katie Turner, Shane Stewart, Courtney McCreary, Jennifer Mixon, and their colleagues at the University Press of Mississippi for bringing this work up to publication standards. Thanks also to Lloyd Gray and C. D. Smith for their kind words in the foreword. I owe special thanks to those who encouraged, reviewed, and criticized various drafts, including Bill Waller Jr., Les Range, the Reverend Dudley Crawford, Alice Perry, Judy Lewis, Jean Medley, Pete Perry, Lloyd Gray, C. D. Smith, and University Press of Mississippi–assigned readers Dr. Brian Pugh and Luther Munford. Luther was also a great help in getting permissions for reprints. Thanks to Beth Butts Hilton, who provided the basic book cover design and map, and designer Todd Lape for his refinements and final book cover. Thanks to Neil White, who not only offered strong encouragement but also considered publishing the book.

Based in large part on my newspaper columns, this book would not have been possible if numerous newspapers had not agreed to publish my early writings (some sporadically) from 1978 to 1980 and my later efforts from 2009 to 2023. These news sources (some now defunct) include the *Northeast Mississippi Daily Journal* (which published nearly all of my columns since the beginning), the Charleston *Sun-Sentinel*, the *Greenwood Commonwealth*, the *Clarksdale Press-Register*, the *Tunica Times-Democrat*, the Tate County *Democrat*, the McComb *Enterprise Journal*, the *Northside Sun* in Jackson, the *Meridian Star*, the *Mississippi Business Journal*, the *Leland Progress*, the *Montgomery Herald*, the *Oxford Eagle*, the *Bolivar Commercial*, the Columbus *Commercial Dispatch*, the *Delta Democrat Times*, the *Daily Sentinel-Star*, the *Panolian*,

Hub City Spokes, the *Union Appeal*, the *Kemper County Messenger*, the *Newton Record*, the *Neshoba Democrat*, the *Starkville Daily News*, the *Madison County Herald*, the *Itawamba County Times*, the Indianola *Enterprise-Tocsin*, the *Madison County Journal*, the *Magee Courier–Simpson County News*, the Kosciusko *Star-Herald*, the *Winston County Journal*, the *New Albany Gazette*, the *Okolona Messenger*, the Biloxi *Sun Herald*, the *Picayune Item*, the *Mississippi Press* in Pascagoula, the *Hattiesburg American*, the *Clarion-Ledger*, the Jackson Jambalaya blog, and the *Magnolia Tribune* online.

Finally, I thank my family, especially my wife, Lynn, for encouraging me and tolerating my obsession.

Credits

"Board Move Surprising" was originally published in the Charleston *Sun-Sentinel* on November 11, 1976. Reprinted by permission of John Wyatt Emmerich, president of Emmerich Newspapers.

"Official Urges GOP to Correct Its 'Anti-Black' Image" by Guy Reel was originally published in the *Commercial Appeal* (Memphis) on November 10, 1981. Reprinted courtesy of the *Commercial Appeal* by permission of Thomas Curley, associate general counsel for Gannett Company, Inc.

"Says Others Lack Backbone, Too" was originally published in the *Clarion-Ledger* on April 24, 1983. Reprinted courtesy of the *Clarion-Ledger* by permission of Thomas Curley, associate general counsel for Gannett Company, Inc.

"A Two-by-Four for Mississippi GOP" was originally published in the June 1983 *NEW ERA* newsletter. Reprinted by permission of Les Range.

"Has Mississippi Forgotten Indivisibility?" was originally published in the *Northeast Mississippi Daily Journal* on December 17, 1992. Reprinted by permission of *Daily Journal–Tupelo*.

"Crawford Made Goat in *Ayers* Case" by Sid Salter was originally published in the *Scott County Times* in July 1994. Reprinted by permission of Sid Salter. ©1994 Good Ole Boys Syndicate, Sid Salter.

SOURCE NOTES

5 **he has recruited the only Black in the State Legislature:** R. W. Apple Jr., "Republican Courts Mississippi Blacks," *New York Times*, August 18, 1975.

6 **And the ironic thing at that time:** Jack Bass, "An Interview with Robert G. Clark," Mississippi Department of Archives and History, Jack Bass/William Winter Oral History Collection, May 13, 1992, 3. https://da.mdah.ms.gov/vault/projects/OHtranscripts/AU751_104030.pdf.

20 **Saying Fordice had "alienated African-Americans":** Stephen D. Shaffer and David Breaux, "Mississippi Politics in the 1990s: Ideology and Performance," paper presented at the American Political Science Association, August 27–31, 1997, Washington, DC.

40 **expenditure rises to meet income:** Jerry H. Tempelman, "Does 'Starve the Beast' Work?," *Cato Journal* 26, no. 3 (Fall 2006): 559–72. https://ciaotest.cc.columbia.edu/olj/cato/v26n3/v26n3i.pdf.

42 **Mississippi now leads the nation:** Charlie Mitchell, "Myths Undermine Any Honest Jobs-Welfare Talks," *Commercial Dispatch* (Columbus, MS), June 14, 2017. https://cdispatch.com/opinions/charlie-mitchell-myths-undermine-any-honest-jobs-welfare-talks/.

49 **Each year, state lawmakers across the US:** Rob O'Dell and Nick Penzenstadler, "You Elected Them to Write New Laws. They're Letting Corporations Do It Instead," Center for Public Integrity, April 4, 2019. https://publicintegrity.org/politics/state-politics/copy-paste-legislate/you-elected-them-to-write-new-laws-theyre-letting-corporations-do-it-instead/.

50 **Mississippi leads nation in filing legislation:** Giacomo Bologna, "Mississippi Leads Nation in Filing Legislation That Other People Wrote," *Clarion-Ledger*, April 4, 2019.

64 **conflict entrepreneurs:** Mona Charen, "Do Americans Even Know How to Agree?," *The Bulwark*, December 13, 2022. https://www.thebulwark.com/do-americans-even-know-how-to-agree/. Mona Charen is policy editor of the online publication *The Bulwark*, a nationally syndicated columnist, and host of *The Bulwark*'s "Beg to Differ" podcast.

64 **Democracy demands an informed electorate:** Ilya Somin, "When Ignorance Isn't Bliss: How Political Ignorance Threatens Democracy," Cato Institute, Policy Analysis no. 525, September 22, 2004. https://www.cato.org/policy-analysis/when-ignorance-isnt-bliss-how-political-ignorance-threatens-democracy#.

67 **Wake up, Republicans:** Stuart Stevens, "Wake Up, Republicans. Your Party Stands for All the Wrong Things Now," *Washington Post*, January 1, 2020.

81 **the appalling silence and indifference:** Dr. Martin Luther King Jr., "Remaining Awake through a Great Revolution," Commencement Address for Oberlin College, Oberlin, Ohio, June 1965. https://www2.oberlin.edu/external/EOG/BlackHistoryMonth/MLK/CommAddress.html.

81 **Mississippi is not merely indifferent to poor people:** Christopher Young, "Poverty Is Not a Crime but This Is Mississippi," *Mississippi Link*, August 18–24, 2022.

84 **routinely violates the constitutional rights:** Equal Justice Initiative, "Justice Department Finds Unconstitutional Conditions at Mississippi Prison," April 25, 2022. https://eji.org/news/justice-department-finds-unconstitutional-conditions-at-mississippi-prison/.

84 **In an era when every topic:** Margaret Talev, "2022's War over Racism," Axios, June 2, 2021. https://www.axios.com/2021/06/02/republican-strategy-culture-war-racism.

97 **Self-centered indulgence, pride, and a lack of shame:** Billy Graham, "My Heart Aches for America," July 19, 2012. https://billygraham.org/story/billy-graham-my-heart-aches-for-america/.

98 **financially unsustainable:** J. B. Clark, "Gov. Appoints PERS Study Commission," *DeSoto Times-Tribune* (Hernando, MS), August 11, 2011.

140 **At a time when companies are clamoring:** Scott Cohn, "America's Worst State for Business: Mississippi Is Cheap, but Its Workforce Weak," CNBC, July 13, 2022. https://www.cnbc.com/2022/07/13/workforce-makes-mississippi-americas-worst-state-for-business.html.

162 **The people are sick:** Chris McGreal, "Poorest Town in Poorest State: Segregation Is Gone but So Are the Jobs," *Guardian*, November 15, 2015. https://www.theguardian.com/us-news/2015/nov/15/poorest-town-in-poorest-state-segregation-is-gone-but-so-are-the-jobs.

175 **The MEC could not get Governor Phil Bryant:** Based on my discussions with MEC board members, 2013–2014.

178 **a case study published by the Aspen Institute:** Vaughn Grisham and Rob Gurwitt, "Hand in Hand: Community Economic Development in Tupelo (1999)," Aspen Institute, February 19, 1999. https://www.aspeninstitute.org/publications/hand-hand-community-economic-development-tupelo-1999/.

INDEX

ABOUT THE AUTHOR

Photo by Bentley Crawford

William Sterling Crawford, the first of three children born to William and Marie Crawford, grew up in Canton, Mississippi. After graduating from Canton High School with honors in 1965, he entered the US Naval Academy. Two years later, as a Superintendent's List scholar, he transferred to the American University School of International Service in Washington, DC. Following a car wreck in early 1970, he returned home, completing a BS in mathematics at Millsaps College in 1971 and a master's degree in education from Mississippi State University in 2001.

In Washington, family friend Bob Montgomery got Crawford a part-time job in the office of Representative John Bell Williams. Representative Charlie Griffin kept him as a legislative assistant. So began his career in government, which would include terms in the legislature, on the College Board, and as deputy director of the Mississippi Development Authority.

In 1970, the late Jack Shearer Jr. talked *Clarion-Ledger* editor Purser Hewitt into hiring Crawford as a reporter. Stops at four more dailies and three weeklies as editor plus sixteen years as a syndicated columnist completed his journalism career. It was interrupted in 1975 and 1979 when he worked in Gil Carmichael's two gubernatorial campaigns.

In 1980, Crawford began a fourteen-year career with the Great Southern National Bank in Meridian, rising to executive vice president. Seeking a more service-oriented vocation, he joined Meridian Community College in 1994 as vice president of community and workforce development. In 2001, with support from the Riley Foundation, he founded The Montgomery Institute, a charitable nonprofit with a regional development mission. He retired as president in 2021.

In 1980, Bill married Lynn Campbell of Columbia, Mississippi. They have two children, the Reverend Bentley Crawford (Sarah Love) and Kate Crawford, plus four grandchildren, Lila, Annie, Luke, and Camp Crawford. Bill and Lynn attend Galloway Memorial United Methodist Church in Jackson.